Father Champlin

on

Contemporary Issues

Liguori
ONE LIGUORI DRIVE
LIGUORI MO 63057-9999
314.464.2500

Imprimi Potest:
Richard Thibodeau, C.SS.R.
Provincial, Denver Province
The Redemptorists

Imprimatur:
Reverend Monsignor John R. Gaydos
Vicar General, Archdiocese of St. Louis

ISBN 0-7648-0123-6
Library of Congress Catalog Card Number: 97-71700

Scripture quotations are from the *New American Bible*, copyright © 1970, 1986, and 1991 by the Confraternity of Christian Doctrine, 3211 Fourth Street N.E., Washington, DC 20017-1194, and are used with permission. All rights reserved.

Excerpts from the English translation of the *Catechism of the Catholic Church* for use in the United States of America, copyright © 1994, United States Catholic Conference, Inc.—Libreria Editrice Vaticana. Used with permission.

Excerpts from the English translation of *Rite of Baptism for Children* © 1969, International Committee on English in the Liturgy, Inc. (ICEL); excerpts from the English translation of *Pastoral Care of the Sick: Rites of Anointing and Viaticum* © 1982, ICEL. All rights reserved.

Parts of the present work were originally published in *Eucharistic Minister*, Celebration Publications, Kansas City, MO. Used with permission.

Cover design by Grady Gunter

Father Champlin on Contemporary Issues

Table of Contents

Preface   vii

Introduction: A More Abundant Life Here and Hereafter   ix

Chapter 1: The First Commandment
Practical Atheism   3
Revelation and Superstition   5

Chapter 2: The Second Commandment
Foul Language   8
The Sacredness of Names   9

Chapter 3: The Third Commandment
Sunday Mass Obligation   12
Work on Sunday   14

Chapter 4: The Fourth Commandment
Laws and Life   19
Taxes   21
Voting   22
Civil War and Immigration   22
Parents and Children   24

Chapter 5: The Fifth Commandment
Abortion   26
Taking Care of Ourselves   28
Protecting the Child Within   30
Concern for Others   31
Caring for the Seriously Ill   32
Death Penalty   33
Assisted Suicide   35
Homicide and Hatred   37

Peacemakers   38
War   38

Chapter 6: The Sixth Commandment
Living Together Outside Marriage   42
Chastity   44
Homosexuality   45
Pornography   46
Genetic Engineering   46
Responsible Parenthood and Birth Control   47
Adultery   48
Sexual Abuse   49
Divorce   50

Chapter 7: The Seventh Commandment
Stewardship   53
Accessibility   55
Animal Rights   57
Gambling   57
Marketplace Practices   58
Profits over People   59
Owners and Workers   59
Developed and Developing Nations   61
Preferential Love for the Poor   61

Chapter 8: The Eighth Commandment
Truth and the Media   64
The Seal of Confession   66
Telling Lies or Speaking the Truth   67
Words That Hurt Others   68
Professional Secrets   69

Chapter 9: The Ninth Commandment
Support for Modesty and Purity   72

Chapter 10: The Tenth Commandment
Pursuing a Career and Nurturing a Family   75
Saving the Earth and Sanctifying Your Heart   77

Acknowledgements   79

Index   81

Preface

Several thousand years ago God gave us the Ten Commandments. Are those ancient rules relevant to our contemporary world?

I think they are.

We now have a very current commentary on these commands in the *Catechism of the Catholic Church*. Does that *Catechism* address the real issues we face in society today?

I think it does.

As one approach to these questions, I offer this book on contemporary moral issues. Today there are many publications dealing with those topics. While most of them are distinctly theological, academic, or technical, my book follows a different path.

Its author is not a moral theologian but a parish priest who has been pastoring people for over four decades.

It treats a large though still limited number of current issues that touch our everyday lives. The introduction analyzes the differences between objective moral norms and subjectively sinful actions. The heart of this volume identifies actual contemporary concerns and connects them with official Church teaching as expressed in the *Catechism* under the umbrella of the Ten Commandments.

It contains not only the *what* of Church teaching, but in many instances offers a brief explanation of the *why* behind Church prescriptions. It sketches particular applications of these teachings to American life and notes significant opposition to some of these norms. It also lists references to the *Catechism* after each chapter, thus facilitating an interested reader's task of locating the original teaching on a particular subject.

Its index will help readers to easily locate answers to their inquiries about contemporary moral issues.

I hope and pray that readers will find these pages engaging, informative, and challenging.

Introduction

A More Abundant Life Here and Hereafter

Before 1960 most American Catholics memorized the following Act of Contrition:

> *O my God,*
> *I am heartily sorry for having offended thee.*
> *And I detest all my sins*
> *Because I dread the loss of heaven and the pains of hell,*
> *But most of all because they have offended*
> *You, my God, who art all good,*
> *And worthy of all my love.*
> *I firmly resolve,*
> *With the help of your grace,*
> *To confess my sins, to do penance,*
> *And to amend my life. Amen.*

This prayer lists the motives—love of God and fear of punishment—that prompt us to pursue virtues and struggle against vices. The perfect motivation behind our behavior, of course, is love of God. If we have a real relationship with the Lord, if we consider Jesus a brother, friend, and savior, if we believe that the Holy Spirit dwells within us, then our hearts embrace attitudes and actions that strengthen these connections, and we shun attitudes and actions that weaken or even sever those connections.

However, many people probably find less pure or imperfect motives more often determine their choices. Fearing the loss of heaven forever or dreading an eternity in hell can push someone to avoid an attractive but wrongful option or to follow a difficult but rightful path.

That venerable Act of Contrition fails to mention a third motive—the desire for a serene and healthy life here on earth and the avoidance of chaotic and destructive living in this world.

Those who struggle with addictive habits understand well this last type of motivation. Recovering alcoholics, for example, experience through right choices a serenity of spirit and healthiness of body, where before through wrong choices they knew mostly inner chaos and bodily deterioration.

Virtues bind us closer to God, assure us of eternal joys, and make our lives more satisfying. Vices, on the other hand, weaken or break our relationship with God, place our hereafter in jeopardy, and ultimately mar the beauty of our existence in this world.

The Nature of Sin

Our discussion now becomes complex and cloudy.

What is sin? Are there actions always and everywhere wrong? Can attitudes or thoughts be evil? How do we relate the responsibility of an objectively bad deed to the highly personal conscience of the person behind it?

Sin happens when we fail to follow the divine imperative within us. God speaking in our hearts commands us to do something and we don't do it; God warns us not to do something and we do it.

That inner voice, message, or judgment is our conscience. It is our most secret core and our sanctuary. There we are alone with God. There the Lord's voice echoes in the depths of our being. We must always obey the certain judgment of our conscience. When we disobey that message, we sin.

This introduces a very subjective element into any consideration of right and wrong actions.

At the same time, there exist deeds that are always good and others that are always bad. Independent of surrounding circumstances and personal motives, these actions are either objectively good and to be encouraged or objectively bad and to be discouraged. For example, to feed hungry people and to heal ailing bodies are objectively right actions. Similarly, to tell lies and to commit adultery are objectively wrong actions.

Sins and virtues are not limited to external actions. Jesus condemned lust and hatred of the heart, and he praised inner forgiveness and faith. Thus he teaches us that our thoughts can be either sinful or virtuous.

The complexity intensifies when we seek to connect objectively good or bad behavior to the person who performs an action.

An Illustration

Since the first century the Catholic Church has declared that every procured abortion is morally evil and objectively wrong. In the words of the Second Vatican Council, "abortion and infanticide are abominable crimes."[1] It teaches that a child has the right to life from its conception. Furthermore, to protect this right and to demonstrate strong opposition to abortion, the Church imposes a penalty of excommunication upon those who commit that crime against human life.

However, my experience counseling women who have had abortions reveals a common phenomenon. The pregnant woman usually must talk herself into judging that an abortion is the only alternative before her. She sees no light at the end of the tunnel and envisions no other possible remedy. Nevertheless, her maternal instincts are so inherently strong that only by convincing herself of an abortion's appropriateness can she move ahead with the destructive action. She imagines that, despite a Catholic upbringing, her conscience approves of the abortion. Objectively speaking, her conscience is in error, but she subjectively judges this to be the right decision.

Afterward, and usually some years later, the same woman frequently experiences regret and remorse. I have heard over and over again these words: "At the time it seemed the right or the only thing to do. Now I know it was wrong."

Did she sin by having the abortion? After all, it was an objectively wrong action. Moreover, the Church has certainly made its position on this matter absolutely clear and has even attached an excommunication penalty to those who formally cooperate in an abortion.

Nevertheless, the Church, as noted above, upholds conscience as the ultimate voice we must follow. The woman's conscience, however mistaken, seemingly endorsed the abortion.

If she did sin, was it a serious, grave, or mortal sin? Was it that bad choice that breaks our relationship with God and with the community of believers?

The Church lists three elements necessary for a sin of a mortal nature: the matter must be serious; the person must have full knowledge or understanding of the action's wrongness; the individual must fully and deliberately choose the wrong act.

In our case under discussion, it would appear that the last two ingredients were at least partially missing. Was she guilty, therefore, of no sin at all? Or did she commit a lesser or venial sin?

This case underscores the complex and elusive task of relating objectively wrong actions to the highly subjective conscience of the person committing those deeds. Ultimately, only an all-wise and all-knowing God can accurately make that connection.

This book does not directly address the issue of personal sin. Instead, the text simply details behaviors that are objectively right or wrong. We leave to our transcendent, loving, and judging God the task of determining whether an individual gains merit or commits sin through a particular action.

Opposition

Sometimes there are disagreements on official Church teachings, both within and outside the Church. When there are numerous and substantial objections to a particular point within the Church, like the teaching on homosexuality, or controversial applications to a specific matter, like nutrition and hydration, this book will briefly acknowledge those criticisms and controversies.

Outside the Church, many people strongly oppose the official teaching contained in these pages. Church positions often seem quite contrary to our current mores. That clash, with its alarming consequences, prompted Pope John Paul II to write his encyclical *The Gospel of Life*, reacting to what he viewed as the culture of death rampant in society today.

Roman Catholics, fortunately and unfortunately, live in this world of ours and its contemporary culture. This is fortunate because Catholics can act as a contrary force to unhealthy trends in the culture (for example, abortion and suicide) and can benefit from healthy trends in the culture (for example, care for personal health and stewardship of the earth).

It is also unfortunate because the impact of our culture is so powerful that these trends usually carry us along in their wake. As a result, we Catholics either consciously or unconsciously absorb the culture's sometimes questionable and even destructive values. For example, surveys indicate that American Catholics' attitudes about abortion and their actions do not differ significantly from the attitudes and actions of most other Americans. Studies also show that a majority of Catholics agree with the legalization of abortion and a proportionate number of Catholics have undergone abortions.

Further Questions

Whether or not readers agree with Church teachings or live them out, at least by their reading of this book they will know clearly what the Church officially teaches. For all readers, however, this book may surface more questions than it answers, for example:

- How responsible are we for actions contrary to objective moral precepts? What are factors diminishing or eliminating personal guilt in particular circumstances?
- When do we say an individual has sinned? Are there degrees of sinfulness? Is there or should there be a connection between committing sin and receiving Communion?
- Have power, money, and pleasure become in fact false gods for citizens of today?
- What lies behind the extremely foul language people use, whether in real life or in movies and on television?
- Is there an obligation to purchase groceries and other necessities before Sunday to reduce required work and foster family renewal?
- If the state or federal government funds abortions, would we be warranted in withholding tax payments?
- Could the death penalty be justified in the United States?
- Was Desert Storm a just war? Vietnam? Korea? World War II?
- Should selective conscientious objection be legalized and alternative community service be required?
- How do parents, family, and clergy best respond to a couple living together before marriage?
- What are the moral dimensions of the rapid growth of gambling casinos on American Indian reservations?

How to Use This Book—and Why

An individual may find reading this book straight through an engaging and informative experience simply because the many topics covered are very real issues facing everyone in our contemporary world. However, those in small-group or classroom settings will more likely wish to work through the text chapter by chapter or a section at a time, with ample opportunity for guided but free-flowing discussions. Others may use it as a reference tool, returning to the volume and its index when in need of information about a particular question.

These pages may appear to present merely a host of dos and don'ts, apparently more don'ts than dos. Nevertheless, the goal of these moral precepts has to do with life—life here on earth and a glorious life still to come. Avoiding sin and pursuing virtue results in happier and healthier lives for all here and in eternal life with God hereafter.

These principles for right living simply apply the teachings and life of Christ to our contemporary society. After all, Jesus is the one who promises a double reward for observing these laws of human conduct:

> "I came so that they might have life and have it more abundantly" (John 10:10).

> "This is the will of my Father, that everyone who sees the Son and believes in him may have eternal life" (John 6:40).

---

1. *Pastoral Constitution on the Church in the Modern World* (Gaudium et Spes), Article 51. From *Vatican Council II: The Conciliar and Post Conciliar Documents,* ed. Austin Flannery, O.P., Costello Publishing Co., Northport, NY, 1975, p. 955.

You shall love the Lord, your God,
with all your heart,
with all your being,
with all your strength,
and with all your mind.
Luke 10:27

Chapter 1
~
The First Commandment

*The Lord, your God, shall you worship
and him alone shall you serve.*
Matthew 4:10

Practical Atheism

Few North Americans deny the existence of God and therefore do not merit the title "pure atheists." However, many in the United States and Canada act as if God does not exist and consequently might be labeled "practical atheists." Either they have no time in their busy lives for God, or they worship false gods, or they consider human beings as quite self-sufficient.

A young married Alaskan woman, raised as a fundamentalist Christian but now inactive, had never been inside a Catholic church much less ever experienced any of its worship services. At a conference required by her employer, she attended a brief Catholic paraliturgical event and heard a priest lecture on stewardship. She felt profoundly troubled when he made this remark: "The average American household spends three times as much annually on gambling as it does on contributions to church."

The young woman later commented: "I immediately thought of the weekend my husband and I visited Las Vegas. We spent a lot of monely there, and we give away nothing now. That was not the way I was raised. We are going to change that."

She and her spouse did change immediately. They began to make regular contributions to charity, although they have apparently not yet found time or need for weekly worship. However, I predict that this change, too, will occur in the near future.

Entering this world as William Franklin Graham II placed a special burden upon the young man with that name. According to *Time* magazine's May 13, 1996, cover story, Franklin, the son of today's most famous preacher, Billy Graham, did not want to be his father's heir and played the prodigal son instead. He fought. He taunted the police with high-speed car chases. He loved firearms, rock music, and hard liquor.

But following those false gods, worshiping at their thrones, left a void within. "Something was missing," he commented. "There was that emptiness you can't explain. There wasn't that joy; there wasn't that fulfillment."

The vacuum led to a conversion of heart and lifestyle, a conversion to the true God. "I put my cigarette out and got down on my knees beside my bed. I was his."[1]

Like many before him, Franklin Graham had found that worshiping created things leaves the inner self unsatisfied. Saint Augustine's oft-quoted acknowledgment is appropriate here: "Our heart is restless until it rests in you."[2]

Baby busters, people born after 1964, form a new generation of seekers. They generally have a hunger for spirituality but no relish for religion. They pray and ponder the deeper issues of life but do not feel drawn very much to organized churches and Sunday services.

Those I have visited with usually believe in God, sense a divine influence on their birth, and vaguely expect some meeting with God after death. But they seldom show any need for the Lord between birth and death. They consider the Creator to be distant and not involved with their day-to-day activities. While serious troubles and major tragedies can shake them, they usually feel self-confident and self-reliant.

Sacred Scripture and our Catholic liturgical tradition take a totally different perspective. We believe that

- everything we possess is from God—our time, talents, and treasures
- God is close to the brokenhearted and near to those who are crushed in spirit
- God tells us to ask for anything we need and answers our prayers
- a first portion of what we receive should be shared with others in need
- coming together for worship publicly acknowledges who God is and who we are

Revelation and Superstition

Just before Christmas, the *Syracuse Herald-Journal* (December 20, 1996) carried an illustrated article from Clearwater, Florida, describing what some saw as a holiday miracle. On the side of the black glass Seminole Finance building appeared a two-story image in rainbow colors resembling the Blessed Virgin Mary. The figure, fifty feet wide and thirty-five feet tall, wore a mantle and had a slightly bowed head. Shades of purple, blue, yellow, and green washed across the mirrored surface and created an image that did bear a close resemblance to traditional representations of Mary, the Mother of Jesus.

A customer noticed this image and contacted the local television station. Its noon news described the phenomenon, and immediately crowds began flocking to the parking lot of Seminole Finance.

Over a two-day span, more than sixty thousand people visited the location. Some wept, others recited the Hail Mary, and still others clutched their rosaries, lighted votive candles, or left flowers before the wall. The outpouring of pilgrims required eighteen police officers to maintain order and guide traffic.[3]

Similar alleged appearances of the Blessed Mother have occurred in many spots across the United States during the past two decades. Are these true revelations from God? Did Mary actually appear? How does the Church officially respond to such remarkable happenings?

In its long history, the Church has repeatedly faced comparable situations and has always reacted with great caution. There are several reasons for this slow pace and real reluctance about lending official approbation to private revelations.

The first motive, of course, is the desire to avoid self-deception. The Church's credibility is undermined if it declares something divine that a later development indicates was merely a human invention or a coincidence.

The Church teaches that there has been no new public revelation since the time of Saint John the Evangelist. Moreover, it declares that we should not expect any. We need no further revelation because in Christ, God has told us everything we need to know for our salvation.

While it is understandable, the anxious desire to experience some new revelation illustrated by people's response to the Clearwater happening is nevertheless spiritually unhealthy. In making this point the

Catechism quotes that wise mystic, Saint John of the Cross. He writes: "Any person questioning God or desiring some vision or revelation would be guilty not only of foolish behavior but also of offending him, by not fixing his eyes entirely upon Christ and by living with the desire for some other novelty."[4]

The Church recognizes that certain private revelations have occurred in its history and proven beneficial to some. Even so, it insists that we need to discern carefully whether or not these proceed from God and thus are truly beneficial for our religious lives. Moreover, no one has any obligation to accept or follow such appearances or the teachings proclaimed in connection with them. These principles provide guidance for people promoting or questioning the numerous private revelations of recent years. Too eager a yearning for such divine manifestations, too swift an acceptance of them, or too obsessive a preoccupation with these appearances comes very close to superstition, an attitude or practice prohibited by the first commandment. That kind of thinking and behavior attaches an almost magical importance to them.

People deeply dedicated to the events and messages of current private or non-approved revelations may bristle at the mention of superstition and magic in connection with such revelations. However, these people probably would concur in the Church's opposition to more blatant forms of superstition or magic.

Even a partial list of superstitious or magical activities is long and covers a variety of activities relatively common today: "conjuring up the dead,...consulting horoscopes, astrology, palm reading, interpretation of omens and lots, the phenomena of clairvoyance, and recourse to mediums" (*Catechism* #2116). So, too, dabbling with the occult and conjuring up the dead, or worse, befriending Satan or demons are both dangerous in themselves and contrary to the true worship we owe only to the Lord. These practices diminish or eliminate the respect that belongs to God alone. They lead us away from the surrender of our future to divine providence that Jesus called for in his preaching.

God revealed the Ten Commandments at a time in history when human beings worshiped a variety of gods. We read repeatedly in the most ancient books of the Hebrew Scriptures that the Lord is one, that God is a jealous God, and that we are not to follow strange or false gods. This commandment seems to be equally relevant today.

Catechism #2083-2141; 65-67

A Look into the Heart

1. Have I given my heart over to another god or gods instead of worshiping the one, true God?
2. Am I too attached to a private revelation and critical of those who question it?

---

1. David Van Biema, "In the Name of the Father," *Time,* May 13, 1996, p. 69.
2. Augustine of Hippo, *Confessions* 1,1,1: *Patrologia Latina,* J.P. Migne, ed., Paris, 1841-1855, 32, 659-661.
3. "In Reflection, Some See Holiday Miracle," *Syracuse Herald-Journal,* December 20, 1996, p. 24A.
4. John of the Cross, *The Ascent of Mount Carmel,* 2,22,3-5, in *The Collected Works,* tr. K. Kavanaugh, OCD, and O. Rodriguez, OCD, Institute of Carmelite Studies, Washington, D.C., 1979, pp. 179-180.

Chapter 2

~

The Second Commandment

You shall not take the name of the LORD, *your God, in vain.*
Exodus 20:7

Foul Language

Four teenagers pulled off the road at Bethany Beach, Delaware, last summer and parked their vehicle in a metered slot just a short walk from the ocean. Their clothes and gear showed that they were ready for a day of sun and fun at the shore.

As the adolescents climbed out of the vehicle, the driver shouted to no one in particular, "Close the G__ d____ side window!"

When his young woman friend asked how to do that, he retorted, "Press the f_____ button on the inside of the door."

This was not a major confrontation, a bitter battle, or a raging conflict. It was a bit of impatience expressed in the common language of our times.

In the April 22, 1995, issue of *U.S. News and World Report* John Leo titled his column "Foul Words, Foul Culture." He bemoaned the gutter language of, for example, the respected television drama *NYPD Blue* and the equally crude terms in current commercials.

Movie moguls and television producers often defend the increasing use of foul language in their films or programs as a mere reflection of society. While that is partially true, they choose to ignore the powerful way in which today's media influence and even create the mores of our contemporary culture.

In either case, Leo regrets that apparently we have now "a culture that celebrates impulse over restraint, notoriety over achievement, rule breaking over rule keeping, and incendiary expression over minimal civility."[1]

That teenage driver is part of this culture. How much did his foul-

mouthed commands reflect today's pervasive culture of instant gratifi-
cation, low-level tolerance, and just-beneath-the-surface anger or rage?

Our Catholic Christian teaching contradicts this prevailing cultural
trend. The commandments, the new *Catechism,* and the Bible point
in a different direction. "You shall not take the name of the LORD,
your God, in vain," declares the second commandment (Exodus 20:7).
The *Catechism* spells out the meaning of this prohibition. The positive meaning is that we must use God's name only for blessing, prais-
ing, and glorifying the Lord. The negative meaning is that we must
not abuse God's name by improperly employing the names of God,
Jesus Christ, the Virgin Mary, or the saints.

The Bible, through the writings of Saint Paul, extends this restric-
tion to other foul or inappropriate words:

> No foul language should come out of your mouths, but only
> such as is good for needed edification, that it may impart grace
> to those who hear....All bitterness, fury, anger, shouting, and
> reviling must be removed from you, along with all malice
> (Ephesians 4:29,31).

> But now you must put them all away: anger, fury, malice, slander,
> and obscene language out of your mouths. (Colossians 3:8).

Saint Paul urges, on the contrary, a positive and proper use of speech.
He exhorts us to say "only such as is good for needed edification, that
it may impart grace to those who hear" (Ephesians 4:29). The apostle
adds, "Whatever you do, in word or in deed, do everything in the
name of the Lord Jesus" (Colossians 3:17).

The Sacredness of Names

Throughout Scripture, God frequently sets aside people for particular
tasks. God highlights each person's unique vocation by changing the
name of the person. For example, Elizabeth's son normally would
have been named for his father Zechariah, but she intervened: "No.
He will be called John" (Luke 1:60).

Puzzled neighbors and relatives knew that none of the child's family members bore the name of John. They thus ignored her directive
and instead asked the mute father what Zechariah wished his infant

to be called. "He asked for a tablet and wrote, 'John is his name,' and all were amazed" (Luke 1:63).

Saul, likewise, became Paul, and Simon, son of John, became Peter.

Both the Hebrew Scriptures and the New Testament stress the sacredness and the significance of an individual's name. Biblical stories reveal that the importance of an individual's name is directly related to the importance of God's name.

When Moses sought from God confirmation of his divinely given mission to lead the Chosen People out of Egypt, he inquired, "'When I go to the Israelites and say to them, "The God of your fathers has sent me to you," if they ask me, "What is his name?" what am I to tell them?' God replied, 'I am who am'" (Exodus 3:13-14). God went on to say, "This is my name forever" (Exodus 3:15).

Later in the same book, God stressed that we should not take God's name in vain and that those who do use God's name in vain will not go unpunished (Exodus 20:1-7).

Clearly the giving of names is an activity associated with divine power. Sometimes the name God gives symbolizes the person's function in God's plan. Simon Peter is perhaps the most familiar illustration.

Jesus said to him, "And so I say to you, you are Peter, and upon this rock I will build my church" (Matthew 16:18). The Greek, Aramaic, and Latin terms for *Peter* and *rock* are closely connected, making Christ's naming of Peter a deft play on words. And more than a play on words, they show Christ's divine power to name a person's role in God's plan.

We read in the prophet Isaiah heartwarming words that many apply to our own individual uniqueness and singular sacredness: "Fear not, for I have redeemed you; / I have called you by name: you are mine.... / You are precious in my eyes and glorious, / and...I love you" (Isaiah 43:1,4).

The Church incorporates that sacred nature of a person's name into its rituals. At the beginning of an individual's Christian life through baptism, the priest or deacon asks the parents, "What name do you give your child?"[2] At the end of life, the Church prays for the dying person: "Lord, Jesus Christ, Savior of the world, we pray for your servant N., and commend him/her to your mercy."[3]

God and the Church judge all names to be sacred and special, including the divine name. The Creator expects us to do the same, using every name only with reverence and respect. The careless and common foul language described earlier in this chapter surely violates that norm of respect and reverence and is therefore improper.

There are other less common but more seriously wrongful forms of speech: direct blasphemy—actual spoken hatred or reproach of God; explicit damnation of another; false oaths; and formal perjury—promising to tell the truth with God as a witness and then deliberately deceiving others with falsehood.

In contrast, common pastoral practice recommends that we whisper prayerfully into the ear of a terminally ill person the sacred name of Jesus, that name by which we will be saved. How different this is from irreverent and disrespectful speech.

Catechism #2142-2167

A Look into the Heart

1. Does my everyday speech generally reflect the foul language of the world in which I live or the biblical teaching that I profess to accept?
2. Are names, both human and divine, important to me, calling forth my respect and reverence?

---

1. John Leo, "Foul Words, Foul Culture," *U.S. News and World Report*, April 22, 1995, p. 73.
2. *The Rites of the Catholic Church,* Vol. I, The Liturgical Press, Collegeville, MN, 1990, p. 394.
3. *The Rites of the Catholic Church*, p. 867.

Chapter 3
~
The Third Commandment

Remember to keep holy the sabbath day.
Exodus 20:8

Sunday Mass Obligation

For the first half of this century, the serious obligation to attend Sunday Mass was quite clear for most Catholics. Missing the weekend Eucharist without reason was a mortal sin, ordinarily requiring confession before Communion could be resumed.

Every Catholic also knew that you missed Mass by not being present for all three of its principal parts: the offertory, consecration, and Communion. For this reason, people were careful to arrive in church at least before the preacher had finished his sermon, and they did not leave until the priest had begun giving Communion.

Being late or leaving early were acknowledged as wrongful actions, but those were considered lesser or venial sins and not worth worrying about. These faults might or might not be mentioned in later confessions.

Those perceptions changed in the second half of this century when the Church altered its analysis of the structure of the Mass. Now instead of the three principal parts, liturgical books emphasize four segments of the Eucharist: Introductory Rites, Liturgy of the Word, Liturgy of the Eucharist, and Concluding Rite. Moreover, the ritual stresses that for liturgical actions, including and above all the Mass, to bear fruit or to work, participants must actively participate with faith and obviously be present from start to finish.

Unfortunately, when these changes were first instituted, some religion teachers and pastoral leaders communicated an impression which many of their young students erroneously interpreted. They falsely translated this instruction into the following moral norm: "I don't have to go to church if I don't feel like it or don't believe in the Mass." Many adults adopted a similar attitude.

Although there were other factors involved in this attitudinal shift, the combined effect created an atmosphere during the eighties and nineties in which many Catholics no longer felt obliged to attend Mass each Sunday. Consequently, today many Catholics miss Mass, often without cause and apparently without guilt.

The *Catechism*, in its treatment of the third commandment, explicitly corrected that misconception. "Remember to keep holy the sabbath day" (Exodus 20:8) is a command to rest and worship, to abstain from unnecessary work, and to praise God in a public way.

The *Catechism* could not be clearer about the responsibility to worship publicly: "The faithful are obliged to participate in the Eucharist on days of obligation, unless excused for a serious reason (for example, illness, the care of infants) or dispensed by their own pastor. Those who deliberately fail in this obligation commit a grave sin" (#2181).

The *Catechism* places this moral teaching in a context, explaining how the serious obligation to attend Sunday Mass flows naturally from many central Christian beliefs:

- The term Sabbath, strictly speaking, means Saturday. Early on, the Church transferred its religious observance to Sunday since Christ rose the day after the Sabbath or on Sunday. Moreover, the Holy Spirit descended upon the apostles on a Sunday.
- The Church has always held up Easter as the feast of feasts, the solemnity of solemnities, *the* feast day. Sundays are considered "little Easters."
- The Church primarily happens, occurs, or becomes whenever we gather for the Eucharist.
- A proper Sunday celebration reminds us of how the Lord rested after creation and how God delivered the Jewish people from slavery.
- Just as the Hebrew Sabbath celebrates the creation of the world, so Sunday celebrates the new creation through Christ's Resurrection.

In addition to these historical and theological reasons, there are several practical motives for regular participation in the Sunday Eucharist.

- Our presence at Mass, linked together with many other believers, gives a great, even if silent, example of faith to those who pass by the church and see the crowd assembled for worship.
- Our own sometimes wavering faith draws strength from those who surround us at Mass. They obviously believe or they would not be present.
- Our mere presence at the Eucharist similarly encourages others in their faith struggle. They also presume that we believe or we would not make the effort to attend Mass.
- God frequently speaks to us through the Scriptures, in the homily, or by the liturgy itself. If we are not at Mass, we simply miss an opportunity for this insightful and supportive message.
- Setting aside for God alone one out of the 168 hours bestowed upon us each week makes a priority statement to others, helps us recognize that the Lord is the giver of all our gifts, and provides us with sixty quiet, reflective, spiritually nourishing minutes to keep our lives in perspective.

An early Church teacher and preacher, Saint John Chrysostom, proclaimed to his listeners:

> You cannot pray at home as at church, where there is a great multitude, where exclamations are cried out to God as from one great heart, and where there is something more: the union of minds, the accord of souls, the bond of charity, the prayers of the priests.[1]

Work on Sunday

Keeping holy the Sabbath has a double dimension: to praise God publicly and to avoid unnecessary work. Avoiding needless labor, however, is the negative dimension of a basically positive injunction.

The Church upholds Sunday not only as a day of worship, but also as "a day of grace and rest from work" (*Catechism* #2184). Following the example of our God who rested on the seventh day from all the work of creation, this commandment enjoins believers similarly to make the Lord's Day a time of leisure.

Those hours of rest and leisure are meant to recreate us physically, emotionally, and mentally. They should bring joy—proper to the Sabbath—into our lives, free us for works of mercy, strengthen relationships within the family and among friends, and provide quiet time for prayer and reflection.

The third commandment prohibits only unnecessary or needless work. Therefore, tasks that serve others and are required for their rest, leisure, or recreation do not fall under that prohibition. In fact, considered as labor for the service of other people, these occupations take on a special kind of virtuous quality.

Thus, for example, those in the food, transportation, and entertainment industries actually enable many to make Sunday a day of grace, rest, and rebuilding.

A half-century ago, some so-called "blue" laws in the United States tried to insure the workless nature of Sundays. Few if any of them remain today, but their purpose essentially was noble.

In our current society, many stores offer twenty-four–hour availability and some explicitly advertise "Open on Sundays." The time pressures on family members in America make individuals welcome or even demand such around-the-clock service. In general, we take this phenomenon for granted.

That cultural trend places an added responsibility upon believers to resist a tendency that makes the Sabbath a business-as-usual day. By carefully arranging, when possible, to shop on the other six days and consciously planning for rest, leisure, and recreation on Sunday, we become ready for the Sabbath to be truly a day of grace.

In the early eighties I spent four weeks lecturing at the Theological Winter School in South Africa. Every weekend my colleague and I had an opportunity to visit a different black township and worship with the residents of those struggling areas. These people lived under the unjust burden of apartheid, frequently experienced the violence erupting from the injustice of their situation, and generally existed under substandard conditions.

Despite those obstacles, they continued to gather for Sunday Mass and to spend the Sabbath in rest. They also used this leisure time to assist the poor, at least those poorer or in greater need. In Soweto, outside of Johannesburg, I was impressed to see a cluster of men, members of the Saint Vincent de Paul Society, meeting before Mass to discuss who required help in their district and how they could assist them. These people clearly understood and practiced the full meaning of celebrating the Lord's Day and keeping the Sabbath.

Catechism #2142-2195

A Look into the Heart

1. Is Sunday Mass central to my life, merely an obligation, or of relative insignificance to me?
2. How well or poorly do I observe Sunday as a day of grace and rest from work?

---

1. John Chrysostom, *De incomprehensibili* 3,6: *Patrologia Graeca*, J.P. Migne, ed., Paris, 1857-1866, 48, 725.

*You shall love
your neighbor as yourself.*
Matthew 22:39

Chapter Four

~

The Fourth Commandment

Honor your father and your mother.
Exodus 20:12

Laws and Life

The tiny teenager had never had a chance. From birth, an incurable condition had doomed her to a short life, stunted growth, and an inability to talk. For over a dozen years, her mother and father surrounded this afflicted child with great love and care, as did her two younger brothers. She grew only to about three feet and communicated solely in nonverbal ways.

The girl finally died at home, cradled in the arms of a devoted nurse who then carried her to her parents in an adjoining room. They took turns gently holding their cherished daughter while the nurse drove to the boys' school, explained the situation to authorities, and asked for the youngsters so she could take them home. Officials frowned and hesitated. State law allowed only a parent or an appropriately designated person to pick up a student. The nurse was neither. Fortunately, common sense prevailed. The principal made an exception and allowed the two boys to leave with the nurse.

The regulation governing release of students at that school has a noble purpose—to prevent child abduction or abuse. But unless the administrator of the law had acted sensibly, it would have caused certain and needless pain for the sake of preventing possible future harm.

The fourth commandment's injunction to show respect for parents extends to anyone who has authority, including teachers, leaders, legislators, and law enforcement personnel, because their authority comes from God. The commandment also enjoins us to obey the laws or regulations that these leaders establish for the common good and the proper carrying out of their functions.

19

However, our nation has become an excessively legalistic society. Since life races on faster than laws can change and laws cannot cover all the varying circumstances of life, matters are more complicated. Our society has so multiplied laws and glorified them that it barely tolerates individual judgment and application.

New York City lawyer Philip K. Howard strongly argues this point in his book, *The Death of Common Sense.* "Making rules as precise as possible has become almost a religious tenet," he maintains. "We have constructed a system of regulatory law that basically outlaws common sense."[1]

Howard cites many practical illustrations to prove his thesis. They range from the frustration Mother Teresa of Calcutta experienced with New York City officials over a home for the homeless to people who need to exceed speed limits on emergency trips to the hospital. "Human activity," Howard asserts, "can't be regulated without judgment by humans."[2]

These notions have practical ramifications for Catholics in the United States. Generally we absorb and tend to accept this national bent for multiplying laws and rejecting exceptions. Moreover, we strictly interpret Church rules that actually flow from a totally different legal approach. The system of ecclesiastical law offers more universally adaptable norms and also readily admits of various excusing causes, dispensations, and adjustments.

Some argue that the Church, too, is legalistic. I would counter that the Church is not legalistic, but some Church personnel may be legalistic. For example, a pastor who automatically refuses to baptize the infant of an unmarried couple or a couple not married in the Church will find no justification for such a strict approach in ritual books or ecclesiastical law. Those regulations are much more general and flexible; the priest here has instead developed his own rigid and specific rules that leave no space for adaptation or judgment.

The paradigm for adult obedience to legitimate authority is the obedience a child owes parents until that child reaches maturity and leaves home. Nevertheless, this required obedience is neither blind nor absolute. Rather, it is characterized by an ability to listen with the heart, which is the meaning of the Latin roots *ob + audire*, from which we get our word *obey.* This listening with the heart is an ability that is incumbent upon both followers *and* leaders. The contingencies of everyday life demand the use of common sense and real charity in the application of human rules. Moreover, in some instances, citizens may even bear an obligation to disobey, to refuse obedience to civil laws or authorities that run contrary to an upright conscience.

Taxes

Americans have a habit of commenting: "There are only two things certain in life: death and taxes." Whatever the accuracy of this aphorism, the fact is that an unexpected letter from the Internal Revenue Service will raise the anxiety level and quicken the heartbeat of many U.S. citizens. When seated before an IRS agent who is auditing their tax returns, people often feel nervous and powerless.

Negative attitudes toward the nation's taxation system interestingly contrast with the *Catechism*'s brief statement about the subject: "Submission to authority and co-responsibility for the common good make it morally obligatory to pay taxes" (#2240). The *Catechism* does not address issues such as improper evasions or legitimate loopholes, nor does it clarify how slight or serious is the obligation. Nevertheless, this teaching means that we practice virtue when filing our returns and writing our checks to cover the amount due. That conclusion may seem strange, but it makes great sense when we consider the many benefits that every citizen receives from local, state, and federal governments.

Bishop Victor Balke of the Crookston diocese in Minnesota has used his payment or, rather, nonpayment of taxes as a means of protesting what he judges are unjust and immoral actions of the federal government. The bishop first withheld his taxes during the Vietnam War. He considered American participation in that conflict wrongful and contrary to his Christian conscience. In a small but tangible step, Bishop Balke expressed his opposition both to the United States' military presence in Vietnam and to funding that operation with tax revenues.

He has threatened a similar measure today in protest against actual and proposed federal financing of abortions for the poor. He also would not hesitate to use his column in the diocesan paper and his other communication vehicles to encourage members of the diocese to do likewise.

Bishop Balke acknowledges that eventually, with its computer tracking capabilities, the IRS will discover his rebellious omission and compel him to pay his bill. "At least," he comments, "I am not willingly paying taxes and cooperating with what I perceive as an evil action." The *Catechism* supports his action, saying that within certain limits we may legitimately oppose the abuse of authority:

> The citizen is obliged in conscience not to follow the directives of civil authorities when they are contrary to the demands of the moral order, to the fundamental rights of persons or to the teachings of the gospel. Refusing obedience to civil authorities, when their demands are contrary to those of an upright conscience, finds its justification in the distinction between serving God and serving the political community (#2242).

Voting

Paying legitimate taxes and serving one's country are clear duties of citizens. So is the exercise of the right to vote. Recently, during major election years, United States Catholic bishops have published informative documents on salient social concerns. These are designed to help Catholics make wise choices in the polling booth.

For example, the 1996 booklet, *Political Responsibility*, carries the subtitle "Proclaiming the Gospel of Life, Protecting the Least Among Us, and Pursuing the Common Good." A few lines from the text nicely summarize a Catholic's obligation: "As citizens we need to face our own public responsibilities: to register and vote; to understand issues and assess candidates' positions and qualifications; and to join with others in advocating for the common good."[3]

Civil War and Immigration

President Alberto K. Fujimori of Peru declared that a central goal of his administration was to eliminate the widespread violence dominating this South American nation. Citizens, he hoped, would eventually be able to drive safely through the countryside and walk securely along Lima's streets—a noble and praiseworthy goal.

At the same time, anti-government forces proclaimed their major objective to be a more just distribution of Peruvian wealth and the alleviation of poverty among its citizens—also a noble and praise-worthy goal.

Unfortunately, in seeking to achieve those aims, both sides caused innocent people to suffer. The government, while incarcerating known or suspected terrorists, unwittingly arrested some who were not terrorists. And on December 17, 1996, fourteen rebels of the Tupac Amaru revolutionary movement forcefully stormed the Japanese Embassy in Lima during a formal party there and held over one hundred innocent persons as hostages. The rebels insisted that the government accede to certain demands before they would release the captives.

Four months later a 140-member government assault team invaded the embassy, rescuing all but one of the 72 hostages and killing all 14 rebels. Three soldiers also died. As often occurs in such civic unrest, innocent individuals suffered.[4]

The Church steers a middle course in these highly complex situations. It upholds legitimate authority and considers respect and submission its due. It also sanctions civil disobedience in certain circumstances. Furthermore, it declares that citizens bear a right and a duty to voice just criticisms of the ruling body.

The *Catechism* goes beyond this, listing five conditions that must all be met for armed resistance to political oppression to be morally acceptable:

1. There is certain, grave, and prolonged violation of fundamental rights.
2. All other means of redress have been exhausted.
3. Such resistance will not provoke worse disorders.
4. There is well-founded hope of success.
5. It is impossible reasonably to foresee any better solution (#2243).

Civil rebellions and sectional wars create another issue covered by the fourth commandment—the obligation "of more prosperous nations...to welcome...foreigner[s] in search of the security and means of livelihood which [they] cannot find in [their] country of origin" (#2241). Both this nation and the Church in the United States have experienced the blessings and the burdens connected with widespread immigration. Every citizen in this country can connect personally in some way with the influx of newcomers to America. From the migration of Europeans a century ago to current border crossers from the

North and from the South, the phenomenon has been constant. In some major cities, the Church offers weekend Masses in as many as sixty different languages, a living testimony of its effort to welcome and serve people from other lands.

Parents and Children

Birth and baptism dramatize the enormous dignity and weighty responsibility of parents. When asked how they feel when their children come into the world, parents usually respond with words describing the gamut of emotions from "ecstatic" to "relieved." They often speak about the event as a miracle.

There are solid theological bases for such a statement and an understandable reason for the jubilation. The Church teaches that God directly creates every soul that enlivens the material body. Conception and birth are a joint venture of the divine Creator and the human parents—a genuine, even if ordinary, miracle.

The infant's baptism is a second miracle of life. Through this simple but wondrous rite the Risen Lord comes to live in a unique manner within the newly baptized person. At the baptism, the Church reminds parents of their awesome duties: they "will be the first teachers of their child in the ways of faith." It then blesses them for this demanding task, asking that, in Christ Jesus, they may also be "the best of teachers."[5]

The *Catechism* asserts that "the family is the original cell of social life" (#2207) and a "domestic church" (#2204). Within this sanctuary, parents, by what they say, do, and are, form their offspring in both natural and supernatural virtues or, to describe it differently, foster the secular and spiritual habits of their children. These include such positive qualities as faith, forgiveness, healthy love of self, and unselfish concern for others. Someone once said that there are two lasting gifts parents can bestow upon their children—roots and wings. I would add a third—embraces.

For their part, children have the duty of obeying their parents just as Jesus did at Nazareth. That responsibility to obey ceases when they leave home. However, the obligation to honor and care for their father and mother continues throughout their lives.

This new combination of independence and yet continued love plays out in many situations:

- In preparing for careers or marriage, adult children should consult parents but need not necessarily follow their judgments or recommendations.
- In everyday living, they need to keep in touch and occasionally visit their parents.
- In the parents' declining years, children bear the responsibility of seeing that their fathers and mothers have adequate care.

With increasing numbers of dependent elderly individuals and declining numbers of income-producing younger people in the United States, this last responsibility has taken on special meaning for both grown children and their contemporary society.

Catechism #2196-2257

A Look into the Heart

1. Can I think of experiences in which the tension between laws and life practically affected me?
2. Do I view paying taxes as a burden to be evaded as much as possible or an opportunity to practice virtue?
3. Did I make an effort to become informed about issues or candidates and did I actually vote in the most recent election?
4. What is my attitude toward persons who have recently immigrated to this country?
5. How well or poorly have I carried out my current duties as parent, child, or both?

---

1. Philip K. Howard, *The Death of Common Sense,* Random House, New York, 1994, pp. 10-11.
2. Howard, p. 12.
3. *Political Responsibility: Proclaiming the Gospel of Life, Protecting the Least Among Us, and Pursuing the Common Good, Reflections on the 1996 Elections by the Administrative Board of the United States Catholic Conference*, United States Catholic Conference, Washington, D.C., 1995, p. 3.
4. "Soldiers Rescue 71 Hostages," and "Captives Told: 'We'll Free You in 3 Minutes,'" *St. Louis Post-Dispatch*, April 29, 1997. *Postnet* http://www.stlnet.com:8080/archives/pdarc. April 29, 1997.
5. *The Rites of the Catholic Church,* Vol. I, The Liturgical Press, Collegeville, MN, 1990, p. 406.

Chapter Five

~

The Fifth Commandment

You shall not kill.
Exodus 20:13

Gospel of Life Issues

Abortion

Pope John Paul II maintains that a current culture of death surrounds us, pervading our attitudes, actions, and laws. He cites abortion and euthanasia as two clear examples. The Church, under his strong direction, has struggled to counteract that pervasive atmosphere by proclaiming its own gospel of life.

A recent abortion issue in the United States illustrates the complexity of this conflict between the culture of death and the gospel of life. Moving to restrict slightly the legal availability of abortions, Congress passed a Partial-Birth Abortion Ban Act, only to have President Clinton veto the legislation.

A subsequent study revealed some alarming figures. Over two-thirds of Americans surveyed did not know what partial-birth abortions were. Moreover, they did not know that Congress had passed a bill to ban them or that the President had vetoed the measure. Finally, the poll also indicated that once people understood what the procedure was, 84 percent opposed it.[1]

In defense of his veto Mr. Clinton argued that the procedure was occasionally necessary for the health of the mother. Afterward, several groups and individuals directly contradicted the assertion that the procedure was at times medically necessary. A respected physicians' organization disputed the statement. So, too, did a husband and a wife who are both involved in pediatrics, he as a neurologist, she as a nurse. This couple labeled Mr. Clinton's defensive explanations as "shameless" and his claim as "patently false."

These spouses speak from experience. Writing in *Commonweal's* August 16, 1996 issue, the nurse described her experience of giving birth to their first child, an infant with Trisomy 18. A person with this chromosomal abnormality cannot live for more than a few hours or weeks outside the uterus.

Doctors who perform partial-birth abortions would have targeted this mother for the same procedure. However, the nurse and her physician husband rejected that option. She writes, "Never once did we consider abortion. We prayed that our beloved child would be born alive and live for at least a brief time. My husband and I were drawn very close as we comforted each other."

The baby, Gerard, was delivered alive.

"He was placed on my chest after the neonatologist examined him, and we held him and gently talked to him. The priest who had married us ten months earlier was there to baptize him. Gerard's lungs and heart were weak. His vital signs slowed until he died forty-five minutes after we met him. The beautiful pictures we took of him are among our most cherished possessions. At the funeral home three days later we were able to hold him again. He was buried next to his grandparents and great-grandparents. We have been blessed with five more children, all healthy."

That couple's decision to forego abortion and choose life has had subsequent positive effects upon their children. The mother notes that they "have internalized our love and respect for Gerard, for all babies, and for persons with disabilities. Every August 2 we celebrate Gerard's birthday and his brief but important life with a birthday cake, a visit to his grave, and a trip to [our favorite pizza-and-play restaurant]."[2] Gerard, the children remark, would have loved that restaurant.

This couple lived out in practice what the official Church has been teaching, particularly in recent years. Pope John Paul II's encyclical letter, *The Gospel of Life*, discusses the value and inviolability of human life: "Human life is sacred because from its beginning it involves the creative action of God and it remains forever in a special relationship with the Creator."[3] The encyclical then establishes an inclusive moral norm: "Nothing and no one can in any way permit the killing of an innocent human being, whether a fetus or an embryo, an infant or an adult, an old person, or one suffering from an incurable disease, or a person who is dying."[4] The Holy Father then specifically applies the general principle: "I declare that direct abortion, that is, abortion willed as an end or as a means, always constitutes a grave moral disorder, since it is the deliberate killing of an innocent human being."[5]

The culture of death and the gospel of life are two trends on a collision course.

Taking Care of Ourselves

A positive understanding of the fifth commandment requires us to take good care of ourselves. This requirement flows from the recognition that life and physical health are precious gifts that God has entrusted to us. The Lord expects that we will use them well, for our own welfare and that of others. The good of this mandate becomes painfully clear when we personally experience the contrary neglect or abuse of life and health.

The overweight corporate executive simply shrugged off clear warnings that chest pains and open heart surgery were giving to him. Compulsive eating habits continued unabated until one afternoon his physician confronted the man: "Either curb your compulsion for food or you are going to die."

The stark admonition finally shattered his complacency. At dinner that evening, conscious of the doctor's orders, he ate a moderate amount. Several hours later, however, an addictive rush came over him, and he swiftly polished off a bag of potato chips. It was only then that he recognized his powerlessness before his compulsion to overeat.

A lawyer sat at the kitchen table reading to his wife excerpts from a book about an unmanaged life, an existence out of control, an attitude of inferiority. "That's me!" he exclaimed.

Unfortunately he was also cuddling a drink, in total denial that addiction to alcohol was an essential part of his problem. It took the loss of his wife, alienation from his children, and near death from drinking before he recognized and no longer denied the core issue.

The single mother, addicted to cocaine, sobbed over the phone to a crisis counselor, "I don't want to do this any more." She had finally seen the destructive effect of her drug habit upon her children and wanted to do something about it.

A clergy person, in treatment for compulsive sexual behavior, has taken to heart these principles:

"I have an addiction. It is not my fault I have it, but this compulsion will also never go away. However, if I rely on God's help and use available support, I can control my addictive urges and become a free person."

Those who find these examples irrelevant, judging that personally they are not compulsive overeaters, alcoholics, drug addicts, or sexually enslaved individuals, might ask themselves: "How am I with candy, peanuts, popcorn, or chocolate chip cookies? Do I eat just the needed amount? Is there a hint of compulsion or lack of control there?" The fact is most people in our world feel the burden of addictions or compulsions, some of which are more serious than others.

The cure is simple to state but difficult to implement:

• Overcome denial
• Be willing to take a step toward recovery
• Recognize the permanent nature of the addictive disease
• Realize one's powerlessness
• Accept the need for God's assistance
• Participate regularly in an appropriate support group

Parishes can be significant partners in this healing, freeing process. Offering church facilities for weekly meetings is an important first step. Occasionally listing the phone numbers of available groups like Alcoholics Anonymous in the Sunday bulletin is another valuable and consciousness-raising measure. Offering homilies once or twice yearly on the spiritual principles behind both the addiction and the recovery speaks simultaneously to the addict and those close to the addict. Arranging for classes or workshops in the parish religious or adult education programs is still another useful action.

Jesus came into the world to save us and set us free. The Eucharist is a most potent means of light and strength for those burdened by compulsions. Christ's presence in Word and sacrament can provide the powerless person with guidance and courage.

For the past thirty years, I have received an annual phone call from a man in California. He reminds me that that particular day is his anniversary of taking a first step toward freedom from alcoholic addiction. An undergraduate student, he came to the rectory for some advice. Despite my youth and inexperience, I detected signs of a compulsive habit and directed him to an Alcoholics Anonymous group. That began his journey toward recovery and freedom, toward good health and individual wellness.

Protecting the Child Within

At Yale University, courses in several departments (not solely the divinity school) address ethical issues on various topics such as reproductive technology, politics, and the marketplace.

The questions are complex, and scholars' views can be quite divergent. Sometimes their opinions, greatly influenced by our contemporary moral culature, clash with convention, attitudes, and thought. For example, one Yale professor bluntly stated: "Reproduction [is] no longer in the hands of God."[6]

Barbara and Ken would react quite strongly to that scholar's assertion. Married a half dozen years, they struggled to start a family. Under the guidance of the local fertility clinic, this couple endured months of emotionally and physically draining experiences. Finally, radiant with joy, they excitedly displayed to relatives and friends a sonogram of the six-week-old child they had conceived.

The parents considered this embryo to be a joint production of three parties. They cooperated with God in creating that new life. Reproduction, according to them, is still in divine hands. Their child arrived prematurely at twenty-eight weeks, weighing a relatively healthy four and a half pounds. Doctors swiftly transferred the tiny one to another nearby hospital that has a specialized unit providing remarkable assistance for such early-born youngsters, many of whom weigh much less.

Official Church teaching offers several moral principles about current medical procedures involving embryos like the one Ken and Barbara conceived. The *Catechism* states that

> Since it must be treated from conception as a person, the embryo
> must be...cared for and healed, as far as possible, like any other

human being. Prenatal diagnosis is morally licit "if it respects the life and integrity of the embryo and is directed toward its safeguarding or healing as an individual...."[7] "One must hold as licit procedures carried out on the human embryo which respect the life and integrity of the embryo and do not involve disproportionate risks for it, but are directed toward its healing, the improvement of its condition of health, or its individual survival...."[8] "Certain attempts to influence chromosomic or genetic inheritance are not therapeutic but are aimed at producing human beings selected according to sex or other predetermined qualities. Such manipulations are contrary to the personal dignity of the human being and [contrary to human] integrity and identity" which are unique and unrepeatable.[9]

Concern for Others

The fifth commandment demands that we display respect for others and even work for their well-being. Not to do so could be seriously wrong. The *Catechism* gives a few examples:

- "Those incur grave guilt who, by drunkenness or a love of speed, endanger their own and others' safety on the road, at sea, or in the air" (#2290).
- Worshiping "physical perfection and success at sports" leads us to prefer "the strong over the weak" (#2289). Those tendencies can cause enormous harm. Thus, an angry parent chastising the Little League youngster who strikes out or makes an error can permanently injure that child's self-esteem and vision of life.
- Drug abuse and illegal drug trafficking are seriously wrong. Health care personnel, teachers, and clergy feel like weeping and may even do so when they encounter an infant or child deeply affected by the parent addicted to heroin or crack cocaine (#2291).
- Organ transplants conform to the moral law and "can be meritorious if the physical and psychological dangers and risks incurred by the donor are proportionate to the good sought for the recipient" (#2296).
- Kidnapping, hostage taking, terrorism, and torture are wrong. Our helplessness in the face of such abductions, the injury to innocent people, and the extraordinary sums wasted on security measures proves that they are "gravely against justice and charity" (#2297).

It seems only a widespread change of human hearts will eliminate the evil of lack of concern for others from the modern scene.

Caring for the Seriously Ill

Grown children often must wrestle with terribly difficult challenges involving aging parents. Questions like these weigh heavily on their hearts:

- Do I bring in someone to help at home because my parents are forgetful or frail, even though one or both resent the suggestion and maintain they can take care of themselves?
- Should I arrange for a move from the homestead to some senior housing or first-level health care institution despite my parents' bitter objections and inability to recognize their own failing condition?
- What kind of extraordinary medical care do I permit for my non-communicative parent whose condition almost certainly will not improve?
- Is it better to bring my parent home and, with hospice help, make it possible for a death in familiar surroundings instead of at the more impersonal hospital?
- May I discontinue the artificial tubular feeding of my parent and allow death to happen, or must I continue this nutrition and hydration through invasive tubes?

Again, official Church teaching offers general guidance in these situations. Those who are sick or disabled deserve respect and the chance "to lead lives as normal as possible" (#2276). Directly ending their lives "is morally unacceptable" (#2277).

The Church also addresses particular issues:

- Even if death is imminent, we must continue to provide ordinary care for the sick.
- We may use painkillers to alleviate the sufferings of the dying, even though this could increase the risk of death. In such a situation we do not will death as an end or a means but rather foresee and tolerate it as inevitable.
- We may discontinue medical procedures that are "burdensome,

dangerous, extraordinary, or disproportionate to the expected outcome" (#2278). If able, the patient should make the decision whether to continue. If the patient is unable, those legally entitled to act for the patient should make that choice, seeking always to respect the patient's reasonable desires and legitimate interests. Ideally, those wishes have been expressed in a health care directive written by the patient while still competent.

The *Catechism* does not specify whether invasive methods like intravenous feeding are ordinary or extraordinary. Nor does it resolve the related and currently much controverted issue about tubular hydration and nutrition. Some argue that we have an obligation to provide water and food as ordinary care; others maintain that use of an intrusive tube to do so is extraordinary care and not obligatory.

In summation, we may use extraordinary means, but there is no moral obligation to employ them. However, while family members may be relieved to know that discontinuing extraordinary treatment is morally acceptable and in accord with Church teaching, their decision to stop such procedures will frequently be heart-wrenching for them.

When the late Cardinal Joseph Bernardin of Chicago struggled with a fatal cancer, he gave dying persons and their families a stirring example. "Death," he said, "can be viewed as a friend or an enemy....As a person of faith, I choose to welcome death as a friend."[10]

Culture of Death Concerns

Death Penalty

The death penalty issue comes before the eyes of Americans on an almost daily basis. Two best-selling books offer significant insights on the topic, John Grisham's novel *The Chamber* and Sister Helen Prejean's *Dead Man Walking*.

Grisham dramatizes the arguments for and against the death penalty and the complexities of that debate. He describes the warden at Mississippi's Parchman Prison:

He hated the death penalty....[But], if pressed, he could make these arguments [for it] as persuasively as any prosecutor. He actually believed one or two of them....But the burden of the actual killing was his, and he despised this horrible aspect of his job.[11]

Sister Helen, an active opponent of the death penalty, describes her involvement with two prisoners on death row at the Louisiana State Penitentiary in Angola. She served as their spiritual advisor throughout those last days, walked with them on their terrible journeys to the electric chair, and witnessed their deaths.

Prejean remains adamantly opposed to the death penalty, but experiences with the families of victims have tempered her views.

> I feel I am still right to oppose capital punishment. But I had not thought seriously enough about what murder means to victims' families and to society. I had not considered how difficult the issue of capital punishment is. My response had been far too simplistic.[12]

In 1980 the U.S. Catholic bishops issued a *Statement on Capital Punishment*. They upheld the long tradition of the Church that the state has the right to take the life of a person guilty of an extremely serious crime. Saint Augustine argued for this position in the fifth century and Saint Thomas Aquinas reasoned similarly in the thirteenth century.

However, the U.S. bishops' statement objected to present death penalty procedures in this nation for, among other reasons, their discriminatory nature, since "those condemned to die are nearly always poor and disproportionately black."[13]

More currently, a good number of individual bishops and clusters of bishops have expressed their objections to capital punishment.

The *Catechism* repeats the traditional teaching that governments have the authority to punish criminals, and that duty may include enacting the death penalty. Is the Church, therefore, strongly in favor of the death penalty? Again, no.

Pope John Paul II in his encyclical letter *The Gospel of Life* acknowledges the right of the state to employ capital punishment. Nevertheless, he cautions that this would be justified only in cases of absolute necessity, in situations in which it would not be possible otherwise to defend society. The Holy Father further comments, "Today, as a result of steady improvements in the organization of the penal system, such cases are very rare, if not practically nonexistent."[14]

What do Catholics in the United States think about the death penalty? In one predominantly Catholic area, a secular newspaper surveyed readers. The study revealed that 66 percent of respondents opted for the death penalty and 26 percent for life imprisonment without parole as the proper punishment for first-degree murder.[15]

Must a Catholic necessarily reject the death penalty? No. As noted above, the Church, in a tradition dating back to at least the medieval period, has upheld the right of individuals and society to use force, even to bring about death, for the sake of legitimate defense. Well-informed, conscientious, and properly motivated Catholics might judge that in today's world the death penalty is a necessary punishment and deterrent for heinous crimes. They may lobby, vote for, and even carry out such capital punishment. On the other hand, those who take the opposite view can cite clear backing of their position by significant persons in the Church—from Pope John Paul II to local bishops.

The Academy-Award–winning film version of *Dead Man Walking* dramatizes the complexity of this controverted issue. It concludes with a view from above of the inert, just executed criminal on his back with arms outstretched in the lethal injection death chamber. It then pans to a similar view of his two brutally murdered victims, their teenaged bodies spread-eagled on the ground in a lonely wooded area.

Assisted Suicide

At the beginning of 1997 two publications both carried substantial articles on the same subject. *Time* reported on "Is There a Right to Die?" with this reading line: "The Supreme Court weighs an issue that may prove to be as contentious—and ethically murky—as abortion rights."[16] *The Philadelphia Inquirer* titled its story, "Agonizing Over Whether We Have a Right to Die" with this reading line: "A hearing on assisted suicide showed a Supreme Court deeply uneasy with the issue."[17]

Laws in the states of Washington and New York prohibiting assisted suicide, later overturned by highly publicized federal appeals court decisions, prompted the Supreme Court action and the simultaneous coverage. In Washington, a ninth-circuit judge voided the state's law, maintaining that choosing a dignified death was a constitutional right and stating that a terminally ill adult should not be compelled to endure a childlike state of helplessness.

Shortly thereafter, the Second Circuit Court of Appeals overruled a similar New York law. It reasoned that if a patient on life support can direct a doctor to pull the plug resulting in the patient's death, then that service should not be denied to a terminally ill patient not attached to a machine.

At least some of the judges in the New York decision saw no distinction between allowing a person to die and directly bringing about the individual's death. That is precisely the difference that the Church insists upon.

According to nationwide polls, a majority of Americans support the decision of the appeals courts. However, a number of doctors, the American Medical Association, other medical groups, and some religious denominations have strongly disagreed with the overturning actions, urging the Supreme Court to review and reverse those judgments in the Washington and New York cases.[18]

The famous Oath of Hippocrates, dating back to Greece in 400 B.C.E., likewise opposes assisted suicide. The oath, so revered by many physicians, includes this promise: "I will not give poison to anyone, though asked to do so, nor will I suggest such a plan."

As it does so often in these contemporary moral concerns, the Church holds a view contrary to that of the majority. The *Catechism* reminds us that "we are *stewards*, not owners, of the life God has entrusted to us. It is not ours to dispose of" (#2280). Suicide is a violation of love of self, others, and God. On the matter of assisted suicide, the *Catechism* teaches quite unequivocally that it is immoral.

At the same time, the Church teaches that various factors can diminish the responsibility of persons committing suicide, that we should not despair of their salvation, and that we pray for (and usually bury) persons who have taken their own lives.

On June 26, 1997, the Supreme Court rendered its decision on the two cases. It did not declare the right to die a broad constitutional right. Instead it unanimously upheld New York and Washington state laws banning the right to die and delegated the matter to individual states for local resolution. Despite this high-level decision, we can expect assisted suicide to be a concern for years to come.

Homicide and Hatred

A winter issue of the *New York Post* carried on its inside pages these stories:

"Delaware prosecutors dropped their objections to bail for eighteen-year-old New Jersey high school sweethearts...who are accused of killing their infant son."[19]

The body of JonBenet Ramsey, a six-year-old beauty queen, was found in the basement of the family's posh Boulder, Colorado, mansion, eight hours after her mother found a ransom note demanding $118,000. "The golden-haired beauty, a former Little Miss Colorado, was bound and strangled."[20]

"You are a murderer! You are guilty as sin! You are a liar! You murdered my husband. Burn in hell where you belong." Those bitter and hateful words were spoken by a widow to the New York policeman whom she claims killed her husband during an altercation that occurred between the two men when the officer attempted to arrest her spouse.[21]

Newspapers in other large cities carry similar daily accounts of violent homicides and hateful attitudes. Contrary to all that are the prohibitions flowing from the fifth commandment. It forbids the deliberate murder of an innocent person as well as indirectly intending murder of another. This includes exposing others to mortal danger without serious reason (for example, irresponsible driving) and refusing to assist a person in danger of death (for example, today's attitude of "I do not want to become involved"). Causing or ignoring widespread famine in a country or area through greed or apathy would likewise come under this prohibition.

Legitimate defense, of oneself or of others, is not only a right but a duty. However, the defense should be limited to only the degree necessary. Police officers generally seek to follow that norm, for example, trying to shoot an assailant in the leg rather than through the heart.

This fifth commandment proscription also extends to the anger that leads to hatred or vengeance. The Lord Jesus takes that a step further, requiring his followers to turn the other cheek and to love their enemies. (See Matthew 5:21-26,38-48.)

Peacemakers

When Michael John returned from Vietnam after serving with the military police there, no one in church welcomed him home, and the congregation did not applaud his return. However, when about the same time another young man returned from Canada, having fled there to escape the draft, he was welcomed in church by name, and the congregation applauded.

The *Catechism* offers insight into these contrasting events. Those who oppose violence without harming the rights of others give witness to Christ's message (#2306). Nevertheless, governments have "the right and duty to impose on citizens the obligations necessary for national defense" (#2310). It praises and calls peacemakers those who serve their country in the armed forces because they contribute to peace and the common good.

Public authorities must also provide an alternate means of service for those who have conscientious objection to bearing arms. In the United States our laws protect such general conscientious objectors—people opposing all wars and arms. Our laws do not, however, extend that alternative to selective conscientious objectors—those who oppose a specific war. The American bishops have been advocating for such a legal provision but currently without success. The *Catechism* does mention, nevertheless, that those who refuse to serve with the armed forces in general or in a specific conflict, must perform some other service.

War

In the introduction we raised questions about certain wars during the past century involving the United States. Were Desert Storm, Vietnam, Korea, and World War II just wars? Years ago our Holy Father visited the United Nations and pleaded: "War no more; war never again." His ardent wishes were not fulfilled. But they did make known worldwide the Church's constant teaching, repeated in the *Catechism*. Everyone must pray and act "so that the divine Goodness may free us from the ancient bondage of war" (#2307). It requires all citizens and all governments to work for the avoidance of war while affirming their right to self-defense.

The *Catechism* then outlines the conditions of just war, conditions that must be considered with the greatest seriousness and that must be fulfilled simultaneously:

— the damage inflicted by the aggressor on the nation or community of nations must be lasting, grave, and certain.
— all other means of putting an end to it have been…impractical or ineffective.
— there must be serious prospects of success.
— the use of arms must not produce evils and disorders graver than the evil to be eliminated. The power of modern means of destruction weaponry weighs very heavily in evaluating this condition (#2309).

Before and after Desert Storm there were and continue to be debates about the application of this "just war" theory to that conflict.

The *Catechism* goes on to offer observations on some quite specific aspects of warfare:

• "Non-combatants, wounded soldiers, and prisoners must be respected and treated humanely" (#2313).
• "Actions deliberately contrary to the law of nations and to its universal principles are crimes, as are the orders that command such actions. Blind obedience does not suffice to excuse those who carry them out. Thus the extermination of a people, nation, or ethnic minority must be condemned as a mortal sin. One is morally bound to resist orders that command genocide" (#2313).
• "'Every act of war directed to the indiscriminate destruction of whole cities or vast areas with their inhabitants is a crime against God and man, which merits firm and unequivocal condemnation.'[23] A danger of modern warfare is that it provides the opportunity to those who possess modern scientific weapons—especially atomic, biological, or chemical weapons—to commit such crimes" (#2314).

The *Catechism* raises serious doubts about the moral validity of deterrence, that is, the accumulation of arms to deter potential adversaries from war.

This method of deterrence gives rise to strong moral reservations. The arms race does not ensure peace. Far from eliminating the causes of war, it risks aggravating them. Spending enormous sums to produce ever new types of weapons impedes efforts to aid needy populations; it thwarts the development of peoples. Over-armament multiplies reasons for conflict and increases the danger of escalation (#2315).

Real peacemaking is the work of eradicating injustice, economic and social inequality, envy, distrust, and sinful pride. In the words of Pope Paul VI, "If you want peace, work for justice."

Catechism #2258-2330

A Look into the Heart

1. If an expected pregnancy with difficult circumstances happened to me or my family, would I consider abortion as a solution?
2. Do I have any addictive habits harmful to me and others? How should I attend to my need for healing?
3. Am I conscious of the truth that each child's soul is God's direct creation?
4. Would I be considered an aggressive, irresponsible, and arrogant driver or an unselfish, careful, and gracious one?
5. What decision have I made about my own end-of-life moments: Sustain me by every means possible or make me comfortable and allow me to die?
6. Which alternative do I favor for the punishment of a very serious crime—the death penalty, life imprisonment without parole, or some other alternative?
7. How do I feel about doctors or health care personnel assisting people to deliberately take their own lives?
8. Have I been holding on to some hatred or resentment toward an individual who has hurt me?
9. Do I show respect for those serving in the armed forces and also for conscientious objectors?
10. Did I consider Desert Storm a just or an unjust war?

1. *Choose Life: A Pro-Life Religious Outreach Newspaper of the National Right to Life Committee*, Washington, D.C., July/August, 1996, p. 2.

2. Margaret Sheridan, "The Veto Was Wrong," from correspondence in *Commonweal*, August 16, 1996, pp. 28-30.

3. John Paul II, *The Gospel of Life: On the Value and Inviolability of Human Life: An Encyclical Letter*, United States Catholic Conference, Washington, D.C., 1995, Article 53, p. 94.

4. *The Gospel of Life*, Article 57, p. 102.

5. *The Gospel of Life*, Article 62, p. 112.

6. Bruce Fellman, "Teaching Ethics in an Age of Ambivalence," *Yale Alumni Magazine*, Summer 1996, p. 27.

7. Congregation of the Doctrine of the Faith, *Donum vitae* I,2, quoted in the *Catechism of the Catholic Church* #2274.

8. *Donum vitae* I,3, quoted in the *Catechism* #2275.

9. *Donum vitae* I,6, quoted in the *Catechism* #2275.

10. Joseph Cardinal Bernardin, *The Gift of Peace*, Loyola Press, Chicago, 1997, pp. 127-28, 135.

11. John Grisham, *The Chamber*, Doubleday, New York, 1994, p. 85.

12. Helen Prejean, C.S.J., *Dead Man Walking: An Eyewitness Account of the Death Penalty in the United States*, Random House, New York, 1993, p. 65.

13. "Statement on Capital Punishment," (November 1980), *Pastoral Letters of the United States Catholic Bishops,* Hugh J. Nolan, ed., Vol. IV, 1975-1983, USCC Office of Publishing Services, Washington, D.C., p. 432.

14. John Paul II, *The Gospel of Life*, Articles 27 and 56, pp. 49-50, 99-100.

15. "Death Penalty for First-Degree Murder," *Syracuse Post-Standard*, August 3, 1994, p. A9.

16. David Van Biema, "Is There a Right to Die?," *Time*, January 13, 1997, pp. 60-61.

17. Michael Vitez, "Agonizing Over Whether We Have a Right to Die," *Philadelphia Inquirer*, January 12, 1997, p. E-1.

18. Carey Goldberg, "Oregon Braces for New Fight on Helping the Dying to Die," *New York Times*, June 17, 1997, pp. A1, A12.

19. "Teens Could Get Bail in Baby Slaying," *New York Post*, January 16, 1997, p. 5.

20. Jackie Rothenberg, "Lab Rat Sold L'il Miss Photos: Cops," *New York Post*, January 16, 1997, p. 5.

21. Rocco Parascandola, "Widow Hounds Livoti," *New York Post*, January 16, 1997, p. 5.

Chapter Six
~
The Sixth Commandment

You shall not commit adultery.
Exodus 20:14

Living Together Outside Marriage

The family life office of a Midwestern archdiocese recently surveyed five hundred engaged couples who had experienced one of the archdiocesan marriage preparation programs. Among other questions, the engaged men and women responded to these two: "Have you participated in sexual intercourse with each other during your courtship?" and "Are you living together now prior to your marriage?" About 90 percent responded "Yes" to the first question and about 40 percent said "Yes" to the second.

Those figures merely confirm similar statistics from around the country. Such data indicate that the number of couples in the United States living together before they marry has geometrically increased over the past two decades.

Apart from the morality of this arrangement, does the practice better prepare the engaged pair for marital life? Scholars who conducted empirical studies when this rapidly growing trend first emerged concluded that indeed living together prior to nuptial vows seemed beneficial for various reasons. However, more current research points in the opposite direction. Several contemporary analyses note that married couples who did not live together beforehand have now scored more positively on some survey questions than those who did live together in advance of the wedding ceremony.[1]

That evidence is not overwhelming, but it does give empirical support to the Church's traditional teaching on the matter. The *Catechism* makes a brief and straightforward declaration about this issue: "The sexual act must take place exclusively within marriage" (#2390).

Why does living together without nuptial vows serve as a harmful instead of helpful preparation for marriage? Here are several possible reasons. Couples living together before the wedding generally tend to

- Avoid discussing tough issues.
- Repress anger at the other's annoying behavioral actions or patterns.
- Continue free spending habits which, while tolerated now, can irritate later in marriage when money will be needed for more critical items like a car, home, or children's education.
- Contend with family opposition to this living arrangement through direct confrontation or evasive dissembling.

How does the Church or, more specifically, how do parish clergy respond to such couples when they connect with a priest or deacon and seek to be married at the altar? Responses understandably vary. Several dioceses established a decade ago rather strict policies that required living-together couples to separate before marriage or, under certain circumstances, to marry but in a quiet, side-chapel setting. Those directives, however, never spread to many other areas.

Most family life offices, recognizing that common residence prior to the wedding is not an impediment to marriage, instead developed a series of questions like these for couples living together:

1. Why did you choose to live together (for example, fear of permanent commitment, testing the relationship, convenience, need for companionship, financial reasons, escape from home)?
2. What have you learned from this experience of having lived together?
3. What is it that is causing you to want to commit yourselves to marriage at this time?
4. Was there a previous hesitation to marry? If so, why? Are you now at a new point of personal development?
5. What is it that prompts you to marry in the Roman Catholic Church at this time? In other words, why have you approached a Catholic priest or deacon now?
6. What does marriage as a sacrament and sacred union mean to you?
7. How do you see your faith and love and the continued growth of

that faith and love for one another as being an intimate part of your marriage?

After reflecting on these questions, some engaged couples have stopped living together. A few, unable to do this because of economic or other factors, have even decided that, as a sacrificial gift to God and as a further preparation for marriage, they would abstain from sexual intercourse until their wedding day. Others, of course, simply continue living together as before.

The *Catechism* bluntly asserts that a sexual act outside of marriage is always wrong and excludes one from sacramental Communion.

Family members and friends, aware of traditional Church teaching and perhaps also personally convinced of its wisdom in this regard, frequently experience great conflict in these circumstances. They wish to show love, support, and compassion for the couple, but at the same time they feel a responsibility to express their disagreement with the living-together arrangement.

Chastity

Robert Farrar Capon is an Episcopal priest who describes himself as a "player of music, teacher of Greek, husband, and father of six."[2] In his book, *Bed and Board: Plain Talk About Marriage*, he offers some advice to couples about chastity before marriage.

Sex before marriage, he maintains, is not the same as sex after marriage regardless of the similarities. The real issue is one of keeping promises. While most unmarried persons wouldn't have sex with anyone other than the one they currently love, later in marriage that may not always be so clear. Chastity now helps promote trust later.

Capon thus counsels individuals and couples: "If you have so far been chaste, don't let anyone talk you out of it. And if you haven't been, well, try and cut out the compromises. Even a tardy dose of principle is better than none."[3]

Starting over again is what some call "secondary virginity." People who take this path need to let go of their regrets about the past, experience God's mercy for previous poor choices, and realize that they may have grown in humility and compassion through their experience. They experience the freedom, peace, and clarity of vision that comes from resuming a chaste life.

Chastity, according to the *Catechism*, integrates our sexuality, unifying us in body and spirit. Sexuality is most deeply and truly human when expressed "in the complete and lifelong mutual gift of a man and a woman" (#2337). Chastity is self-mastery or training in human freedom. This virtue, which is for all the baptized, single and married, teaches us to find peace by controlling our desires. Without it, we live unhappily at the mercy of our passions. Self-knowledge and self-discipline as well as the exercise of virtue and faithfulness to prayer help us find the peace that comes from living chastely, something we must strive for daily.

Homosexuality

On December 4, 1996, a Honolulu circuit-court judge ordered Hawaii officials to stop denying marriage licenses to same-sex couples. However, he put a hold on implementation of his decision while the state appealed it. Several religious groups, including many evangelicals, Mormons, and Muslims, condemned the ruling. Other religious groups, including some Reform Jewish leaders and pro-gay organizations within mainline denominations, applauded the mandate.[4]

Where does the Church stand on this issue?

While the *Catechism* does not explicitly mention same-sex marriages, its teaching on homosexuality clearly prohibits them. It cites the Catholic tradition based upon Scripture that homosexual acts cannot be approved under any circumstances. But it then urges compassion toward those with homosexual tendencies. We must avoid discrimination against homosexuals and respectfully accept them as people who, like all Christians, have a vocation and who are called to chastity.

Gay rights proponents will likely consider this teaching unacceptable and even offensive. Many active homosexual persons will also find the words hard to hear and harder to follow. The legal question of same-sex marriages will no doubt continue with us in the United States for some time. The struggle of homosexual persons to understand, accept, and follow the Church's teaching will also remain in the spotlight for years to come.

Pornography

The Spitfire Grill, a charming movie about life in a small rural New England community, won the Audience Award at the Utah Sundance Film Festival shortly after its release. The film was made in a distinct way:

There are no explicit sex scenes.

The central characters rarely, if ever, use foul language.

Violent conflicts in the movie have an intense but restrained character to them. They are real-life struggles but not the gory incidents we have come to expect in current films.

The noble intent and tone of *The Spitfire Grill* contrasts with today's pornography, which can be blatant or subtle. Pornography is not limited to hard-core movies or magazines. The messages and images of television sitcoms and first-run movies may exert an equally potent pornographic impact on the viewer's mind.

The *Catechism* considers pornography an offense against chastity. Pornography perverts the sexual act and offends human dignity by making sexuality a means of immoral pleasure and monetary profit (#2354).

Today's widespread discussion about regulation of the Internet, movies, and television to curtail the impact of pornography, especially upon the young, underscores the need to control the availability of pornographic material.

Genetic Engineering

In his recent novel *The Third Twin*, best-selling author Ken Follett dramatizes the scientific marvel and moral riskiness of genetic engineering. The main plot is a clandestine effort to clone perfect American soldiers. Scientists fraudulently implant "perfect embryos" in some unsuspecting mothers. When these clones reach adulthood, a major moral issue surfaces—ancestral confusion. One of the soldiers, upon learning about his origin, anguishes about his lack of normal human ancestry.[5]

Follett's novel arrived in bookstores only a few months before Dolly, the first cloned lamb, appeared on the front page of daily newspapers. Her appearance triggered enormous discussion among scientists, legislators, and moralists around the world about the ethical issues involved in potential human cloning.

The *Catechism* states that

> techniques that entail the dissociation of husband and wife, by the intrusion of a person other than the couple (donation of sperm or ovum, surrogate uterus), are gravely immoral. These techniques...infringe the child's right to be born of a father and mother known to [the child] and bound to each other by marriage (#2376).

The Church does not universally condemn all forms of genetic engineering, since many of the techniques are life-saving and do not violate the principles stated above. However, this section of the *Catechism* (#2376) implies condemnation of cloning, since cloning does involve asexual reproduction, the creation of a new individual from a single body (somatic) cell. The clone is therefore genetically identical to its only parent—the donor of the single cell. We can expect to hear much about cloning and other forms of genetic engineering in the years ahead.

Responsible Parenthood and Birth Control

Michael and Pamela married when he was twenty-eight and she was twenty-four. Like many couples, they felt a need to postpone children for a short period of time. Pamela explains: "I talked to my doctor about the pill. But when he explained to me the possible side effects, I thought that there had to be something better, something approved by the Church. We called our priest, invited him to dinner, and hit him with the rough, heavy question of birth control. He connected us with a doctor and his wife who were instructing others in Natural Family Planning (NFP)."

They attended the classes, began to practice NFP, and used the system to avoid pregnancy. Later they used it to encourage their first pregnancy. Her doctor was quite surprised when, armed with charts and figures, she announced to him that she was pregnant. And she was.

Now in their forties with three children, Mike and Pam continue to practice and preach NFP. Their age, experience, and example add credibility to claims that this Church-approved method for regulating births has many beneficial effects. These include deepening marital intimacy, more effective religious training of children, and healthy attitudes toward sexuality.

The Second Vatican Council's notion of responsible parenthood should guide spouses in spacing the births of their children. That means recognizing the unique blessings of large families, avoiding selfishness, and trusting in God's providence, but at the same time using human reason and will to decide the question of when and how to have children.

In carrying out this judgment, the *Catechism* considers that periodic continence (abstinence from sexual intercourse) is a licit means of spacing births and contraception is not, because all marital acts must be open to the transmission of life, which contraception makes impossible (#2366, #2370).

In recent years the popes and the American bishops have encouraged couples struggling with this challenge of properly spacing children to have faith, to pray and trust, to never grow discouraged by their weakness, and to approach the sacraments of reconciliation and Eucharist frequently for guidance and strength.

Adultery

Through the Old City of Jerusalem runs the Via Dolorosa (Sorrowful Street) along which Jesus stumbled on his way to Calvary. From antiquity most buildings in that area have had a flat rooftop area with apartments, gardens, and a clear view of other homes. The Notre Dame de Sion retreat house is no exception. Standing on its roof and looking over the neighboring roofs makes the story of King David's adulterous relationship with Bathsheba come alive: "One evening David rose from his siesta and strolled about on the roof of the palace. From the roof he saw a woman bathing, who was very beautiful" (2 Samuel 11:2).

The king made inquiries about her and discovered that she was the wife of Uriah the Hittite. Despite this knowledge, David summoned her and had sex with her. This led to deceit, more abuse of power, the arranged murder of her husband, and other wrongdoing. "The LORD was displeased with what David had done" (2 Samuel 11:27).

How many times has this scenario been reenacted since that famous incident centuries ago? The *Catechism* contains few but potent words about adultery as an offense against the dignity of marriage (#2380, 2381).

Adultery or marital infidelity occurs when two people, of whom at least one is married to someone else, have sexual relations. Christ denounced even the wish to commit adultery, and the prophets saw it as a symbol of idolatry. The offending spouse injures others in breaking a marital commitment and in so doing undermines the institution of marriage, jeopardizing the proper nurture of children and their right to a stable home.

Sexual Abuse

About ten years ago, the bishop of an Eastern Canadian diocese brought all his clergy to a retreat house on the outskirts of Ottawa, shutting down operations in his diocese for two weeks. That bishop took such a radical step in an attempt to rebuild the shattered morale of those parish priests and to renew their appreciation of the priesthood.

His diocese and the entire Canadian Catholic Church had been devastated months before through very public disclosures of sexual abuse allegedly perpetrated by the clergy. This dark cloud hovered over Canadian Catholics for several years and then, like an Arctic storm, moved south, crossed the border, and spread over the United States.

The sexual abuse epidemic, or at least the public revelation of and response to it, has brought enormous pain and harm to the Church. But even more horrendous are the scars and wounds that its victims bear. The injuries endured, especially by youthful victims, include:

- The violation of trust. In most instances, the perpetrators are persons in a loving, close, and trusting relationship with the victims. Sexual abuse is usually inflicted by adults on young people who know and rely upon them in some way. That betrayal causes enormous conscious and unconscious confusion, doubt, and anger.
- The creation of a false but profound and painful guilt. Just as little children often falsely blame themselves for the discord and marital breakup of their parents, so, too, youthful victims tend to assume responsibility for the abuse.
- The poisoning of attitudes toward relationships. Victims, deeply tortured by self-doubts and false guilt, frequently struggle with their relationship to God. They also often have difficulty relating on an intimate level with another person, erecting overt and subtle barriers

to ward off possible intimacy. The victims may likewise find themselves uncomfortable with sexual relationships, especially with their spouse.

• The infliction of permanent damage. The *Catechism* states that the young will remain scarred by it all their lives. Even with successful therapy, victims, much like persons with addictions, sense that the wounds are always there, healed a bit but ever ready to bleed again and stir up painful memories and emotions. They move on and manage their lives, yet remain aware of the deep scars.

Clergy sexual abuse has undermined the reputation of the clergy. Even though a minor percentage of cases are clergy related, the publicity given sexual abuse incidents involving priests, especially, because of their spiritual calling and local prominence, makes this problem seem much more widespread. It has also discouraged innocent clergy and made them feel defensive, awkward, and inhibited when dealing with people, particularly children and teenagers. It has spawned countless costly lawsuits with settlements leaving some dioceses and individuals practically bankrupt.

In both the Church and society at large, sexual abuse has led to the institution of procedural norms that, for example, restrict or eliminate physical contact, limit one-on-one pairings, and change traditional patterns of association between adults and young people. While these rules are designed to protect the innocent and defenseless young, they frequently wound innocent and caring adults and deprive young people of natural contact with them. As one forty-seven-year-old veteran first-grade teacher said, "When children come up and spontaneously hug me, I'm going to continue to return those hugs. But I worry now about what might happen."

A central and common response of both the Church and society is one of compassion for victims of sexual abuse and their families. Sympathetically hearing stories of sexual abuse and then responding with appropriate assistance is a start. It helps facilitate the healing process and begins to repair some of the damage done.

Divorce

One very popular marriage preparation speaker quickly gains the attention of his listeners with this statement: "You guys and gals, men and women, I am splitting this audience down the middle aisle. Half of you couples are on one side of this aisle, the other half are on the opposite side. Here is my prediction: half of you will have successful marriages, and the other half will see your marriages fail."

This fact about the divorce rate is true and well known, but his blunt prediction still stuns them. However, he quickly softens his harsh prediction with a promise: "If you spend five minutes every day communicating personally, listening to one another with love, then I guarantee you will succeed in marriage."

Christ taught that marriage is indissoluble: "What God has joined together, no human being must separate" (Matthew 19:6). The *Code of Canon Law* states that for Christians, "A ratified and consummated marriage cannot be dissolved by any human power or for any reason other than death."6 In some complex legal or political situations, the Church will tolerate civil divorce, because the Church still regards the civilly divorced spouses as truly sacramentally married and expects them to behave as such.

Divorce is harmful because it breaks the contract of lifelong fidelity between spouses, and it may harm children who are often torn by the conflict and separation between their parents. The *Catechism* is careful to stress the distinction between an innocent spouse unjustly abandoned and one who is responsible for destroying a valid marriage (#2386).

The pastoral care of separated and divorced Catholics is an important issue. It includes the process of acquiring official declarations of nullity that free contracting parties to marry again. It also includes counseling and other kinds of support. The process of going through a divorce may generate feelings of self-recrimination, rejection, self-doubt, hostility, and confusion. Parish clergy and pastoral ministers in this country expend enormous time and energy caring for those affected by divorce. They seek to help the healing process, enabling those wounded by marital separations to learn from their experiences, move beyond their scars, and begin new lives.

Catechism #2331-2400; #1628-1629; #1649-1651

A Look into the Heart

1. Do I think that the practice of couples living together before marriage is right or wrong, good or bad, and why?
2. How does the quest for chastity fit into my life?
3. Am I in favor of same-sex marriages or opposed to them and for what reason or reasons?
4. Have I become so accustomed to the frequent pornographic element in television and movies as to miss its destructive and manipulative impact?
5. What do I judge to be some of the positive and negative aspects of genetic engineering and, in particular, of cloning?
6. How have I or would I practice responsible parenthood with regard to the spacing of children?
7. Can I recall incidents in fiction or fact that illustrate the hurtful effects of adultery?
8. Do I think the names of alleged sex offenders should be made public while the identities of the alleged victims are concealed?
9. What do I think has caused divorce to become so common in this country?

---

1. Bishops' Committee for Pastoral Research and Practices, *Faithful to Each Other Forever: A Catholic Handbook of Pastoral Help for Marriage Preparation*, National Conference of Catholic Bishops, Washington, D.C., 1988, pp. 71-77.
2. Robert Farrar Capon, *Bed and Board: Plain Talk About Marriage*, Simon and Schuster, New York, 1965, book jacket.
3. Capon, pp. 22-24.
4. "Clash Over Gay Marriage," *Christian Century*, December 18-25, 1996, p. 1246.
5. Ken Follett, *The Third Twin*, Crown Publishers, New York, 1996, p. 310.
6. *Code of Canon Law*, Canon Law Society of America, Washington, D.C., 1983, canon 1141.

Chapter 7

~

The Seventh Commandment

You shall not steal.
Exodus 20:15

Good Use of Our Gifts

Stewardship

During 1994, Catholic households gave an average of $508 to their churches and charities. In contrast, those with no religion donated $848, Protestant homes contributed $969, and households of other religions averaged $1,406.[1] In 1991 the average income for a Catholic household was $40,903, while the average income for the typical American household was $37,922.[2] Consequently, although the annual income of a typical Catholic household exceeds the annual income of the average U.S. household, the total charitable donations of Catholics lag significantly behind the similar contributions of all other Americans.

Most bishops in southern and southwestern dioceses would immediately create many new schools and parishes to meet the rapidly expanding Catholic populations in the Sunbelt—if they had the financial resources and the personnel. Large parish churches, formerly staffed by several priests, now struggle along with one, who, with paid and volunteer helpers, must care for the spiritual needs of an equal- or even greater-sized flock.

Church leaders recognize the need to pay just salaries, sustain or expand Catholic schools, provide quality music for liturgies, sustain and develop first-rate religious education programs, serve the poor, maintain buildings, plan for future major physical plant repairs or expansion, and still contribute not only their financial surplus but also their substance to developing countries overseas. Yet they must do so with fewer clergy and more limited financial means.

Some solutions to these problems seem likely to come from two sources: one is the average actual income of American Catholics; the other is the burgeoning use of lay persons, paid or volunteer, to collaborate with the clergy in their service of parishioners. Two well-publicized contemporary success stories indicate that it is possible to tap the enormous treasure, time, and talent of U.S. Catholics and to direct those resources to the task of building up the Church and making this a better world.

Father Tom McCread has been pastoring Saint Francis of Assisi parish in Wichita, Kansas, for two decades. His longtime commitment to stewardship has produced remarkable results: a weekly Sunday collection of $50,000-$60,000; over 2,000 volunteers engaged in a wide diversity of ministries serving both parishioners and the city's poor; free Catholic education; around-the-clock Eucharistic adoration; and substantial crowds at daily Masses.

Another success story is Sacrificial Giving. Over 2,000 parishes in the United States and Canada have implemented this program. With lay testimonies, a biblical base, and spiritual orientation, it has produced an average increase in weekly contributions of 45 percent. Those figures have been realized in totally different economic, geographical, ethnic, and pastoral settings—a testimony to the universal value of this concept. It has also stimulated a variety of parish volunteer or stewardship weekends. Those experiences annually secure the services of hundreds—men and women as well as boys and girls—who are quite willing to offer their gifts and energies for the parish and its programs.

The American bishops have developed a philosophical or theological base for such distinct but similar enterprises. Their 1992 pastoral letter, *Stewardship: A Disciple's Response,* and 1996 resource manual, *Stewardship and Development in Catholic Dioceses and Parishes,* offer general concepts and practical suggestions for such efforts.

This excerpt captures the essence of the bishops' pastoral:

> Disciples who practice stewardship recognize God as the origin of life, the giver of freedom, the source of all they have and are and will be....They know themselves to be recipients and caretakers of God's many gifts. They are grateful for what they have received and eager to cultivate their gifts out of love for God and one another.
>
> Who is a Christian steward? One who receives God's gifts

gratefully, cherishes and treats them in a responsible and accountable manner, shares them in justice and love with others, and returns them with increase to the Lord.[3]

In concert with this teaching, the *Catechism* says that God has blessed us and made us stewards of the earth. This responsibility entails working for a just distribution of resources for all people. It especially enjoins property owners to use their wealth for the good of those entrusted to them and for the benefit of others: "The ownership of any property makes its holder a steward of Providence, with the task of making it fruitful and communicating its benefits to others, first of all [the owner's] family" (#2404). "Goods of production—material or immaterial—such as land, factories, practical or artistic skills, oblige their possessors to employ them in ways that will benefit the greatest number" (#2405).

Accessibility

Many years ago Katherine Jensen taught public speaking and drilled teenagers in debating techniques. Now nearing ninety, she recently captivated a huge congregation by her magnificent proclamation of a reading from Jeremiah. Because of her short stature, Katherine stood on a box placed behind the lectern so she could see and be seen by participants. All—including the bishop—listened attentively, fascinated by her age, her dignified approach, and her careful rendering of the Word.

Those who approach the altar for Communion at Saint Lucy's Church frequently receive the Lord from a hearing-impaired person. That eucharistic minister holds a vessel of consecrated hosts in the left hand and signs "The Body of Christ" with the right, then removes a host and presents it to the communicant.

Kathy O'Neill walks in the entrance procession at Mass with her hand on a companion's arm. Later the same partner escorts her to the pulpit where she opens up a brown booklet. Then, using that Braille text, she clearly and carefully proclaims the readings of the day to the people. As this young woman, sightless from birth, speaks God's Word to the people, their hearts are uniquely touched.

The residents at Rosewood Heights Nursing Home assemble weekly for Mass in their recreation room. Mostly older persons, although several are relatively young, they all share the same burden. Their bodies, either through advancing age or debilitating disease, have deteriorated.

Some sleep through the Mass. Others need a reminder to open their mouths to receive the host. Still others no longer speak but can only express their willingness, faith, and gratitude at Communion through a gesture or a smile.

John Bateman-Ferry became a paraplegic after an accident in his late teens. Despite the obstacles, he finished college, learned to navigate by wheelchair and specially constructed van, married, had three children, and became executive of an advocacy agency.

John also serves as a lector. But to enter the sanctuary to proclaim the Scripture readings, he must take a circuitous route through the parish office and sacristy. Even then he cannot actually reach the pulpit but reads from his movable chair, holding a microphone in one hand and the Scriptures in another.

In their pastoral statement on persons with disabilities, the U.S. bishops write, "It is essential that all forms of the liturgy be completely accessible to persons with disabilities....Realistic provision must be made for persons with disabilities to participate fully in the Eucharist and other liturgical celebrations."[4]

In a 1995 document containing guidelines for celebration of the sacraments for persons with disabilities, the bishops repeated this significant principle: "Cases of doubt should be resolved in favor of the right of the baptized person to receive the sacrament."[5]

As a Church we have done fairly well making the sacraments available to all. This is but one way, albeit a significant one, by which the Church models principles of accessibility for the world. We still have work to do in making liturgical ministries equally open to everyone.

The *Catechism* extends this ideal of accessibility to the marketplace and secular life. It states that no one—including people with disabilities—should be subject to unjust discrimination in employment.

Animal Rights

The February 1997 issue of *Scientific American* featured two comprehensive and conflicting articles on animal experimentation. In the first article, two practicing physicians argued that "animal research is wasteful and misleading....While using animals may prove intellectually seductive, these tests are often inapplicable to humans."[6]

Two university professors wrote the second article, arguing that "animal research is vital to medicine" and has "played a crucial role in the development of modern medical treatments."[7]

Animal rights activists obviously side with the first position. Their convictions lead them to protest before medical colleges, picket clothing stores that sell fur coats, and demand vegetarian meals at banquets.

What does the *Catechism* teach on this topic?

As God's creatures, animals are intended to be used for the good of human beings. For our part, we may use animals for food, clothing, work, leisure, and reasonable experimentation, but we must do so only out of a deep respect for the integral whole of creation. We must keep our relationship to animals in perspective, treating them with kindness and respect, but not devoting to them resources that are needed for human beings.

These principles will likely spark sharp comments from people on opposite sides of the animal rights controversy.

Gambling

In chapter 1, the section on practical atheism tells the story of a young woman and her husband who, on a weekend vacation to Las Vegas, gambled away a considerable sum of money. Their experience is that of many people around the country. So popular is the new Foxwoods Casino in Connecticut that special buses link the New London train station with the casino.

A large number of casinos have sprung up during the past decade across America, most drawing huge crowds that wager substantial sums on slot machines, cards, and other games of chance. But gambling is not something new to the United States. Catholic churches have for years sponsored bingo and bazaars, multiple raffles and Vegas Nights. Betting on horse races, Sunday professional football contests, and the World Series is commonplace. State-run lotto or lottery chances offer incredible prizes for lucky winners. The inclination to gamble apparently runs deep within our human nature.

What does the Church have to say about gambling? Gambling is not in itself morally wrong. Card games, bingo, or wagers like baseball and football pools do not in themselves offend justice. However, it is unjust and irresponsible to gamble money needed for one's support and the support of dependents. Moreover, gambling easily can become an addiction. Cheating at games or making unfair wagers are also wrongful actions, the seriousness of which is determined by the harm done. Because of these dangers, some bishops have prohibited Church-sponsored gambling within their dioceses.

Marketplace Practices

Over a period of a year, the film series director at a middle-sized Midwestern university embezzled $29,000. One day, as he was walking down the hall, he saw two police officers coming toward him. Sensing that they were there to arrest him, he walked up to them and, without introduction, said, "I'm glad you finally came."

Apart from how crushingly such actions may weigh on the individual conscience or how often we hear of such crimes, stealing or theft is wrong. The *Catechism* specifies actions that constitute theft or stealing—some obvious, others more subtle, some direct, others indirect, but all contrary to the seventh commandment. These include:

- deliberate retention of goods lent or of objects lost
- business fraud
- paying unjust wages
- forcing up prices by taking advantage of the ignorance or hardship of another
- speculation in which one contrives to manipulate the price of goods artificially in order to gain an advantage to the detriment of others
- corruption in which one influences the judgment of those who must make decisions according to law
- appropriation and use for private purposes of the common goods of an enterprise
- work poorly done
- tax evasion

- forgery of checks and invoices
- excessive expenses and waste
- willfully damaging private or public property (#2049).

Changing Structures to Build Solidarity

Profits over People

A decade ago, corporate executives in New Jersey decided to close their century-old plant in a neighboring state. It employed around fifteen hundred people and had been a very profitable operation.

But situations change. The fiscal bottom line was no longer as attractive; other alternatives existed; the corporation could move the production process elsewhere and gain a higher return on its investment. While the fate of those employees and of that community posed some concern for corporate leaders, profit issues dominated their decision-making.

The *Catechism* takes a dim view of a profit-centered approach to life and to social structures. Human beings are much more than simply a means of profit. Valuing money before people is immoral and the cause of tremendous social and political ills. Neither pure socialism nor pure capitalism can bring about social justice, because true human needs transcend ideologies and economics. Instead, economic activity must be subject to a system of moral values, most especially justice. The desire and need for profits may be legitimate, but to sacrifice, neglect, or injure people in the pursuit of them runs contrary to God's plan for us (#2423-2425).

Owners and Workers

In 1986 the American bishops issued a lengthy, profound, and controversial document, *Economic Justice for All*. On the tenth anniversary of this pastoral letter, the U.S. bishops produced a summary statement, *A Catholic Framework for Economic Life*, which contains ten points as principles for reflection, criteria for judgment, and directions for action. Number 5 declares that

all people have the right to economic initiative, to productive work, to just wages and benefits, to decent working conditions, as well as to organize and join unions or other associations.

Number 9 states that

workers, owners, managers, stockholders, and consumers are moral agents in economic life. By our choices, initiative, creativity, and investment, we enhance or diminish economic opportunity, community life, and social justice.[8]

The authors acknowledge the *Catechism* as a source, particularly in its treatment of the seventh commandment under sections "The Social Doctrine of the Church" and "Economic Activity and Social Justice." Those two sections contain general but practical norms:

- Because economic life inevitably involves conflict, negotiations to reduce those conflicts are morally obligatory and should engage all interested parties. A peaceful strike for just reasons is morally acceptable when other means of conflict resolution have been exhausted. Strikers and management must avoid violence.
- Workers deserve a just wage, and employers who withhold it may be guilty of a serious injustice.
- The principal task of the state is to guarantee "individual freedom and private property,...a stable currency, and efficient public services" (#2431). The government may legitimately require social security contributions.
- Unemployment almost always harms workers and their dependents.

For example, two decades ago I lectured at the Theological Winter School in South Africa and its neighbor, the tiny, impoverished kingdom of Lesotho. Opportunities for work in Lesotho were very limited. To obtain employment, many husbands and fathers lived in South African cities for lengthy periods of time—six months or a year—sending home money for the family. Such an existence created enormous individual stress, moral risks, and domestic dangers.

Developed and Developing Nations

Some globally conscious and generous parishes practice something like the following. Each weekend they deduct a tithe or 10 percent of their Sunday collection and place it in a fund for the hungry, homeless, and hurting. They note that deduction in the weekly bulletin and invite members to submit the names and background information of individuals or groups who are serving the poor outside the parish limits. These potential recipients may be anywhere—in the local area but not within the parish, in the diocese, in the U.S., or beyond our borders.

Every three months a small parish committee evaluates the requests for funds and allocates most of the accumulated money. They divide these donations evenly between recipients within the diocese, elsewhere in the nation, and outside the United States. They request an acknowledgment from each recipient with, ideally, photos describing their efforts to help the hungry, homeless, or hurting. They post the responses on a mission board in the vestibule, a visible testimony that the parish possesses a universal vision of the Church and a generous heart that responds to current needs everywhere.

Advocates of this process will find great support in the *Catechism* in the section entitled "Justice and Solidarity Among Nations." The gap between rich and poor nations is a worldwide social problem requiring the efforts of rich nations to effectively and justly foster the development of poor nations. This help must take the form of reform of unjust systems, just and charitable economic practices, and direct aid followed by efforts to bring about permanent change. This obligation is especially binding with regard to the Third World poor.

Preferential Love for the Poor

Reverend Richard Allen Bower serves as dean of Saint Paul's Episcopal Cathedral in Syracuse's center city. Like the spiritual leaders of most mainline Christian churches in urban areas, he struggles to accomplish three main tasks: to maintain a beautiful but older and expensive-to-operate physical plant; to serve a declining flock brought about by the flight of so many to the suburbs; and to work effectively with the hurting people who assemble in great numbers and diversity around downtown churches.

More than one hundred homeless and hungry people line up outside Saint Paul's each afternoon for a hot meal at the Samaritan Center. The center gives witness to Father Bower's love for the poor.

But his concern for those in need extends beyond this upstate New
York neighborhood. In the fall of 1966, he traveled to Central America
and for four months lived with and listened to the stories of war, loss,
and healing among the people of El Salvador. In 1993 he again visited El Salvador to establish an ongoing relationship between the
Episcopal dioceses of Central New York and El Salvador. He and his
colleagues believe that such a companion relationship would be valuable for both dioceses.

Upon his return, Father Bower commented that "solidarity with
the poor and the oppressed is walking the same journey with them,
sharing the same struggles, while charity is loving from a distance."[9]
He also believes that a prophetic church must not only practice charity to the poor and oppressed but must also move beyond to address
the underlying causes of poverty and oppression. "We need to be part
of the transformation of society as well as being part of the compas-
sionate response. Compassion is not enough."[10]

The authors of the *Catechism* would applaud his example. They speak
about the poor in very moving terms: "Love for the poor is incompat-
ible with immoderate love of riches or their selfish use" (#2445). They
remind us of the words of Saint John Chrysostom: "Not to enable the
poor to share in our goods is to steal from them and deprive them of
life. The goods we possess are not ours, but theirs."[11]

They also call us to practice the traditional spiritual and corporal works
of mercy (among which are comforting, consoling, forgiving, feeding
the hungry, sheltering the homeless, and clothing the naked). They
stress the preferential love of the Church for the poor, citing Saint
Rose of Lima: "When we serve the poor and the sick, we serve Jesus. We
must not fail to help our neighbors, because in them we serve Jesus."[12]

Catechism #2401–#2463

A Look into the Heart

1. Are my contributions for church and charity off-the-top, ten-
   percent, sacrificial donations made in gratitude to God? Or do I
   give simply what is left over out of habit?

2. How do I feel and react when I meet persons with disabilities?
3 What is my attitude toward gambling and perhaps my practice of it?
4. Am I for or against the use of animals for food, clothing, and medical or scientific experimentation?
5. Have I slipped into some bad personal or marketplace practices that constitute a form of stealing?
6. Is my personal life and work in the marketplace excessively profit centered?
7. What are my experiences of corporate downsizing, unexpected layoffs, unemployment, and labor-management disputes?
8. Am I in favor of assisting people overseas? Or do I think the adage "Charity begins at home" justifies limiting assistance to my near neighbors or fellow Americans?
9. Would I characterize myself as having a preferential love for the poor?

------

1. "Who Gives What," *U.S. News and World Report*, December 4, 1995, p. 87. Compiled by Anna Mulrine, Basic Data: Giving USA 1995, American Association of Fund-Raising Counsel.
2. Joseph Claude Harris, *An Estimate of Catholic Household Contributions to the Sunday Offertory Collection During 1991*, Life Cycle Center of Catholic University of America, Washington, D.C., December 1992, pp. 12-13.
3. National Conference of Catholic Bishops, *Stewardship: A Disciple's Response*, United States Catholic Conference, Washington, D.C., 1996, pp. 1,7.
4. *Guidelines for the Celebration of the Sacraments With Persons With Disabilities*, United States Catholic Conference, Washington, D.C., 1996, p. 1.
5. *Guidelines for the Celebration of the Sacraments With Persons With Disabilities*, p. 5.
6. Neal D. Barnard and Stephen R. Kaufman, "Animal Research Is Wasteful and Misleading," *Scientific American*, February 1997, pp. 80-82.
7. Jack H. Botting and Adrian R. Morrison, "Animal Research Is Vital to Medicine," *Scientific American*, February 1997, pp. 83-85.
8. National Council of Catholic Bishops, *Tenth Anniversary Edition of Economic Justice for All: A Catholic Framework for Economic Life*, United States Catholic Conference, Washington, D.C., 1996, p. 2.
9. Melanie Gleaves-Hirsch, "Driven by Faith," *Syracuse Post-Standard*, March 1, 1997, pp. B1-B2.
10. Gleaves-Hirsch, p. B2.
11. John Chrysostom, *Hom. in Lazaro 2,5: Patrologia Graeca*, J.P. Migne, ed. (Paris, 1857-1866) 48, 992.
12. P. Hansen, *Vita mirabilis*, Louvain, 1668.

Chapter Eight

~
The Eighth Commandment

You shall not bear false witness against your neighbor.
Exodus 20:16

Truth and the Media

On a wintry Friday night, Lori Branche and her fiancé Michael Panasci, both pharmacists, left different workplaces, met, and made their way in her car to a local sports bar. There they watched an exciting NCAA final play-off contest won by the local university's basketball team.

While watching the game, Lori, a very responsible young woman, had one beer and perhaps sipped part of another. When she and Michael left the tavern, the weather and driving conditions had soured. Windblown snow impaired visibility and ice-covered spots made the roads slippery.

At the city's outskirts, Lori lost control of the car on the slick road. It spun around and into the path of an oncoming vehicle. The collision injured Michael and Lori but not seriously. However, it devastated the occupants of the other car. Carmen Rojek was racing to the hospital with his wife, expecting her momentarily to deliver their third child. The impact left him relatively unharmed but killed his spouse instantly. Emergency workers quickly extracted Mrs. Rojek and rushed her to the emergency room where doctors performed an emergency Caesarean section, delivering the infant. Unfortunately, the prolonged lack of oxygen had badly damaged the child, who died nine days later in a neonatal intensive care unit.

The incident traumatized Lori Branche. Dealing with the accidental death of a pregnant woman and her child was bad enough. But newspaper and broadcast news stories during this period reported frequently that a woman charged with drunken driving was involved in an accident that killed a mother and her newborn son. The public accusation of drunk driving greatly intensified Lori's grief and anguish. Numerous nasty calls and even death threats forced her to disconnect the telephone.

Two weeks after the accident, the local newspapers, to their credit, ran fresh stories with a banner headline: "Driver Wasn't Drunk." One article explained: "Blood tests show that Lori Branche, 24, had a blood-alcohol level of 0.03 percent—three times below the legal limit—when her car collided....The legal [limit for blood alcohol] for driving while intoxicated is 0.10 percent. The blood test results do not support the initial DWI charge."[1]

It was too little too late. Her lawyer observed, "How do you dig out from that kind of publicity until the facts are known? It's easy to say, "I wasn't drunk." It's easy to say, "I'm not at fault," but once you're accused of something most people feel otherwise—especially when there is a tragic death like this, two deaths really."[2]

This incident is typical of media reporting that actually ruins the reputations of people. The articles may include disclaimers, and later stories many contain denials or corrections. But usually the damage has been done. Years from now, some will probably whisper about Lori, "She was the drunken driver who killed the pregnant woman and her child."

In its treatment of the eighth commandment the *Catechism* issues some contemporary cautions on this very topic. Readers and viewers need to be less passive and more vigilant about what they see or hear. Wisely discerning the truth and not too swiftly accepting impressions is an ongoing task.

Journalists have a special responsibility to serve the truth through conscientious reporting while always recognizing the inherent limits of reporting, especially where individual persons and the tendency of others to make judgments about them are concerned. The challenge the *Catechism* offers to journalists is to serve the truth with charity. The venerable motto, "All the news that is fit to print" should not be replaced by "Any news that will attract additional readers."

Public servants have special duties in regard to telling the truth. They are commissioned to protect the right of citizens to their reputations and to their privacy. They also must never use the media—or any other means of communication—to misrepresent the truth in order to sway public opinion or gain political or personal advantage.

If American politicians applied these principles to their campaigns and to their conduct of office, they might bring about real and lasting good for all of us.

The Seal of Confession

In the days of black-and-white films, Alfred Hitchcock produced *I Confess,* a Canadian-based thriller involving a priest and a murder. The movie begins with silent action—the assailant making his way late at night through the city, the victim being murdered in bed, and a priest strolling down the aisle of his church. We next see the priest surprised and somewhat annoyed by the perpetrator's bizarre demand to confess at this late hour. However, the priest agrees, enters a pre–Vatican-II–style confessional, and frowns as the man whispers, "I have just killed a man."

Through a complex sequence of events, the innocent confessor is charged with the murder and tried. The prosecutor besieges him with questions. Responding to any of them with the truth about the confession incident would have immediately proven his innocence. However, he repeatedly replies to those inquiries with only this incriminating statement: "I cannot say."

Eventually acquitted, although still publicly judged guilty, the priest emerges from the courthouse to face an angry crowd. The crazed killer reappears, fires off a shot seeking to kill the priest, misses, and takes off. After a mad chase, the killer, believing the priest has betrayed him, shouts out the details of his earlier confession. Suddenly the mystery is solved, the priest cleared, the truth evident.

I first viewed that film over forty years ago in the seminary as a student preparing for the priesthood. I can recall even now the strong feelings it evoked within me about the "seal of confession"—the duty of the confessor never to reveal anything about someone's confession—and what that would mean in my future life as a priest.

The *Catechism* (#1967, #2490) stresses the sacred nature of the secrecy that surrounds the sacrament of reconciliation. The knowledge a priest gains from a penitent is "sealed" by the sacrament, without exception. The *Code of Canon Law* declares that "the sacramental seal is inviolable; therefore, it is a crime for a confessor in any way to betray a penitent by word or in any other manner or for any reason."[3]

Telling Lies or Speaking the Truth

In 1996 Congress passed a law prohibiting partial-birth abortion only to have it vetoed by the President. Opponents of this legislation depended heavily upon the testimony of Ron Fitzsimmons. Fitzsimmons heads the National Coalition of Abortion Providers, a group of 200 clinics that performs abortions. He said at the time of the legislative debate that such late-term abortions were done rarely and only to save a woman's life or abort a badly deformed fetus.

Months later, in early 1997, Fitzsimmons told the press, "I lied through my teeth."[4] He admits now that the procedure is done routinely on healthy women with healthy fetuses in the fifth month.

Many legislators had believed his lies. President Clinton explained his veto in language almost identical to Fitzsimmons' testimony.

Why did Fitzsimmons lie? He said that he did not want to "stir up the pot" while Congress argued the question. He "feared the truth would damage the abortion cause."[5]

Why did he now admit to lying, despite the fact that his admission would likely refuel the controversy, give support to opponents, and perhaps resurrect the legislation? Fitzsimmons replied, "We just felt it was time to be totally candid."[6]

This remarkable admission dramatizes the clear teaching of the *Catechism* on truth and falsehood.

- It quotes the definition of Saint Augustine: "A lie consists in speaking a falsehood with the intention of deceiving."[7]
- It relates lying to truth.
- It explains the essential evil of a lie.
- It provides a guide to determine the gravity or seriousness of a particular lie, which depends on several things, most importantly the importance of the truth that is being distorted and the harm that the lie causes.
- It sketches the harm done by lying. A lie undermines trust and tears apart the fabric of social relationships.
- It details the obligation to repair the harm done. Even if forgiveness has been asked for and received, the author of the lie must repair any harm done insofar as that is possible.

Applying these various principles about lying to the Fitzsimmons incident is an instructive—if sad—exercise.

Words that Hurt Others

A Green Journey and *Dear James*, novels by Jon Hassler, tell the story of Agatha McGee, a conservative semi-retired parochial school teacher from Minnesota, and James O'Hannon, pastor of a church in County Kildare, Ireland. Agatha and James both subscribe to a Midwestern Catholic periodical and both write letters to the editor expressing traditional ideas and attitudes about the Church, which leads them to begin a long correspondence with each other. Unaware that James is a priest, Agatha begins to feel tenderness and affection for him. On pilgrimage in Ireland she meets James and, realizing that he is a priest, she draws back from the friendship and returns home terribly troubled.

Meanwhile, a mean-spirited acquaintance of Agatha's, Imogene Kite, discovers the correspondence and, distorting the real nature of Agatha's relationship to James, slanders them in a taped interview. Another acquaintance, French, is an unwilling accomplice in this evil action. Too weak to stop the deed, he sadly observes the inevitable injury to Agatha's reputation: "He imagined once again how he might have preserved the purity of Miss McGee's name by snatching the master tape away....It made him sick to think of it copied and spreading through town, irretrievable as gossip."[8]

This story illustrates the teaching of the *Catechism* about respect for another's reputation, clearly demonstrating the harm our words can do to others. It teaches that

- We must never, through either word or attitude, unjustly hurt the reputation of another.
- We must see each other in a favorable way whenever possible and avoid judging one another rashly.
- We must avoid detraction, that is, "without objectively valid reason, disclos[ing] another's faults and failings to persons who did not know them" (#2477).
- We must avoid calumny, that is, "by remarks contrary to the truth, harm[ing] the reputation of others and giv[ing] occasion for false judgments concerning them" (#2477).

I have read this section of the *Catechism* perhaps a dozen times. Each reading makes me uneasy, aware of how easily we may slip especially into rash judgment and detraction, the two things that are the ordinary—and uncharitable—substance of gossip. The Epistle of James states, "No human being can tame the tongue" (3:8). It teaches that a person without fault in speech is a person in the fullest sense, able to control her or his entire body.

Professional Secrets

In April of 1995, a bomb blew up the Oklahoma City Federal Building, killing 168 people. Investigators eventually arrested Timothy McVeigh and accused him of involvement in this deadly attack. During preparation for McVeigh's trial nearly two years later, the alleged theft and publication of confidential information complicated the possibility of just and fair treatment by a jury.

The *Dallas Morning News* first in its online and then in print editions published confidential documents allegedly describing McVeigh's confession of the horrendous bombing. His lawyer responded by accusing the *Morning News* of breaking into the defense team's computer system and stealing thousands of sensitive documents including this confession. However, the attorney also stated that this was a hoax confession, designed to persuade a reluctant witness to testify on behalf of the defense.

The incident provoked nationwide debate about the ethical behavior of both the newspaper and the defense lawyer. The American Bar Association states that it is unprofessional for a lawyer to "engage in conduct involving dishonesty, fraud, deceit, or misrepresentation."[9] The former president of a defense lawyers' organization asserts that disbarment would be likely if any of this confidential material was leaked to the newspaper by a member of the defense team.[10]

Newspapers today regularly print material from classified documents they have obtained, if they judge that the newsworthiness of the documents demands it. In the aftermath of the 1971 Pentagon Papers, the Supreme Court reaffirmed a newspaper's right to do so.

Critics of the *Morning News*, however, question the way in which they secured the confidential texts, whether they are actually legitimate documents, and the potential harm such publication might have done to the trial. The publication of the documents might have so seriously interfered with the pretrial and trial process that neither McVeigh nor the 168 victims would have received justice.[11]

The *Catechism* takes very seriously the issue of professional secrets, that is, confidential information that people have because of their work or professional responsibilities. Unless serious harm could be caused by keeping such information confidential and the harm can only be avoided by revealing it, such professional secrets must be kept.

Charity requires us to have respect for people's private lives. Respecting others' privacy in the way we speak about them and to them is a powerful way to observe this teaching. This respect for individual privacy should weigh heavily with communication leaders who must balance that concern with a concern for the common good when revealing information.

It sometimes seems that our contemporary culture has become careless about confidentiality. In such a culture the commandment "You shall not bear false witness against your neighbor" is a rich resource for us, serving us well as a means of deciding every day how to act justly and lovingly toward others.

Catechism #2464-2513; #1467

A Look into the Heart

1. Am I too passive or accepting and not vigilant enough about what I see, hear, or read?
2. Do I have total confidence in the seal of confession?
3. Are there instances in which I have injured another or been wounded myself by a lie?
4. Does my unfortunate personal experience confirm the words of James (3:8) that "no human being can tame the tongue"?
5. How well in my professional and personal life do I keep secrets?

---

1. Jon Craig and Amber Smith, "Crash Kills Pregnant Woman and Baby," *Syracuse Herald-Journal*, March 23, 1996, pp. A1, A2, A12.
2. Jim O'Hara, "Driver Wrestles with Accusations, Tragic Accident," *Syracuse Herald-Journal*, pp. A1, A10.
3. *Code of Canon Law*, Canon Law Society of America, Washington D.C., 1983, canon 983. See also canon 1388.

4. Cal Thomas, "Pro-Choice Forces Lying," *Syracuse Herald-Journal*, March 6, 1997, p. A19.

5. Thomas, p. A19.

6. Mimi Hall, "Partial-Birth Abortions Routine, Backer Now Says," *USA Today*, February 27, 1997, p. 1A.

7. Augustine of Hippo, *De mendacio* 4,5: *Patrologia Latina*, J.P. Migne, ed., Paris, 1841-1855, 40, 491.

8. Jon Hassler, *Dear James*, Ballantine Books, New York, 1993, p. 299.

9. Martha T. Moore and Tony Mauro, "A Question of Ethics," *USA Today*, March 5, 1997, pp. 1A-2A.

10. Moore and Mauro, pp. 1A-2A.

11. Moore and Mauro, pp. 1A-2A.

Chapter Nine
~
The Ninth Commandment

You shall not covet your neighbor's wife.
Exodus 20:17

Support for Modesty and Purity

Technology has transformed television dramatically since its early days. We have swiftly moved from black and white to color, from three network stations to unlimited cable channels, from power and volume controls on the set itself to remotes that enable us to flip from program to program and to raise or lower the sound without stirring in our seats.

The content transformation has been equally radical. Only a few years ago, depictions of violence and sex were restrained and foul language was seldom used. For decades Clark Gable's utterance of "damn" in *Gone With the Wind* was a famous exception to that pattern.

Today violence is commonplace and gory; nudity and sexual actions are explicit; every coarse expression occurs in most television programs. Producers and directors have pushed the envelope in terms of violence, sex, and language.

Parents, educators, and experts in family life are increasingly alarmed about the impact on children of this constant and easily available fare. Their concerns have even led to legislation aimed at protecting youth and providing parents with some control over television.

President Clinton signed the Telecommunications Act of 1996, which included a provision that by 1998 all newly manufactured television sets with screens that are thirteen inches or larger must include V-Chip technology. The law requires television producers to create a message or content ratings scale so that each program will have an electronic code sent over the air or through the cable system along with the program. In the home, the V-chip device can be set to receive certain codes and reject all others, providing a measure of domestic control.

The *Catechism* gives support to such an effort. A healthy modesty, it asserts, protects against the influence the media can have on us in the current climate of voyeurism and exhibitionism.

Modesty counteracts our tendency to covet or desire wrongfully another person's spouse or possessions. Christian theology defines this desire as contrary to reason. In itself it is not wrong, but it can lead to wrongdoing. Every person can testify from human experience the struggle to curb those unruly desires. Modesty helps in that struggle, particularly in the area of sexual covetousness.

The *Catechism* sketches some of the characteristics of modesty. While modesty takes different forms in different cultures, it is the expression of chastity (whether in a married or a single person) because it shows reverence, respect, and reserve toward what is most intimate in human beings. The love of human beings for each other is mysterious and powerful. Modesty helps us to protect the sacredness of human love, to be patient and moderate in our loving, to avoid unhealthy curiosity, and to give to ourselves and to others the respect that is appropriate to our dignity as daughters and sons of God.

The *Catechism* also criticizes advertisements that use sex and the human body to attract customers. Feminists and others who oppose sexual stereotyping would agree with that criticism. Such advertising demeans the human person by reducing individuals to objects and by eliminating the relationship component from sexual actions.

Preserving or regaining sexual puritiy is a challenge, especially for young people today. They need, of course, to develop and maintain an inner and outer modesty. But young people also deserve support for this struggle, support that comes from proper instruction in purity, from prayer, and from a purified social climate, including less manipulative advertising.

With these and other helps, especially God's grace, people can achieve true freedom of the heart and an overwhleming vision of the divine presence.

Catechism #2514-2533

A Look into the Heart

1. Are there ways I have fostered or undermined modesty?
2. Do I think parents and educators should give young people specific, supportive guidance about sexual purity?

Chapter Ten
~
The Tenth Commandment

You shall not covet...anything else that belongs to [your neighbor].
Exodus 20:17

Pursuing a Career and Nurturing a Family

Vincent Smith and Jane Brown, after fifteen years of marriage, made revolutionary adjustments in their lifestyles, shifts that they judged essential for their survival as a couple and for the well-being of their children.

After college and specialty training, Vincent joined a large corporation that provides services across the country. His climb up the corporate ladder was steady but not meteoric; the demands upon him were significant but not all-consuming; ugly downsizing passed him by, but so-called rightsizing has stretched his time and energy resources.

Now nearly forty, he naturally speculates about his future career. How much higher can he climb, how much progress can he anticipate, how much more income growth can he expect?

After nursing school, Jane worked at a local hospital, bore two children, and then joined a dozen physicians in their new private practice office. Unlike Vincent, her rise there was not gradual but rapid. Soon administrator of this large operation, she found the challenges exciting and affirming, but the time and energy demands were exhausting.

All the ingredients now existed for a disaster to happen.

Her long hours and his erratic schedule meant that two very fatigued spouses barely saw each other and seldom had time, the frame of mind, or suitable circumstances to communicate on any deeper level. Distance, resentment, and misunderstanding began to flood their relationship.

However, it was the children's severe emotional problems that brought this unhealthy condition to a crisis point. Counselors and doctors indicated that their school-age child suffered from acute depression, anxiety syndrome, Attention Deficit Hyperactivity Disorder, and dyslexia. The younger one, in nursery school, displayed antisocial behavior, had become quite withdrawn, and possessed more than the usual amount of separation anxiety. Some difficulties were biological in origin but they were exacerbated by the parents' stress and absence.

After months of professional counseling with the children and all the enervating tensions that were accompanying their situation, the Smiths decided that they needed to make a radical change. Jane would take an extended leave of absence from work and become a full-time homemaker and mother. There were unsettling questions connected with this major move.

Could they handle it financially?

Before Jane had gone to work years earlier, the couple had estimated they needed only $200 a month beyond Vincent's salary to meet expenses. Moreover, the added cost required because of Jane's working—baby-sitting, clothes, transportation, eating out—consumed the greater part of her salary. The fiscal gap was, consequently, not as enormous as expected.

Would she be happy full time at home?

This question of vocation is perhaps the most important one, a question unique to each person. It deserves the careful consideration of everyone, since our answers determine how we give daily expression to God's life and love. For Jane, the need for additional money was not the primary motivation for working outside the home. Cultural pressures to have a career outside the home, the excitement of the marketplace, career fulfillment, and the development of personal gifts were strong factors. But the price she paid for these benefits was one she judged as too high.

Would it make a difference to the children's well-being?

The improvement in their children's behavior everywhere was instantaneous and remarkable. They clearly were and are thrilled to have Mom at home and their parents more in love with each other.

Would they have to give up things?

Some things, yes. Their lifestyle is now a bit simpler but still very comfortable. They have learned to distinguish between needs and wants. The children seem to have the hardest adjustment to make. Our consumer culture and its constant advertising understandably affects these two youngsters and their neighborhood friends. The boy and girl, therefore, occasionally wonder why they cannot get a popular item that friends have recently acquired. But their children, too, are slowly learning the many values of simpler living. Moreover, they have no desire to return to life the way it was.

Vincent and Jane exemplify the challenge facing many couples today—to balance the successful pursuit of their careers with the proper nurturing of their families.

The tenth commandment speaks to some of the difficulties people have with this complex issue, since it deals with our tendency to covet material things. Our desires, originally good and related to fostering life, may lead us to become unreasonably attached to things that do not belong to us, things that belong to or are owed to others.

The tenth commandment strongly encourages us to avoid greed, avarice, and envy. As children of God, our real happiness does not lie in merely collecting things for their own sake (greed), grabbing riches and power as ends in themselves (avarice), or inordinately desiring what belongs to someone else (envy). This teaching and the positive charity it implies can serve as guidelines for all of us in making financial, career, and lifestyle decisions.

Saving the Earth and Sanctifying Your Heart

On the east and west coasts and everywhere in between, people have designed a multitude of programs to "Save the Earth." In California, folders in the rooms of one motel chain urge guests to join their water conservation efforts. It gives practical suggestions to help save the state's limited water supply. At Boston's Park Plaza Hotel, the bathrooms have unique fixtures designed to eliminate the use of two million plastic containers annually. McDonald's, which originally bucked environmentalists, has now moved ahead with its own massive "Earth Effort," using its recycled paper bags to describe its conservation program to customers, including the use of one hundred million dollars' worth of recycled products per year.

Those who work at saving this earth for tomorrow's inhabitants cultivate the poverty of heart that the *Catechism* urges. They avoid adherence to riches and instead work to free themselves from a disordered desire for the pleasure of power and riches. Their motivation may be earthbound—seeking a better planet for themselves and for those to come. But the Creator promises a heavenly reward for such an attitude.

The poor in spirit, people who strive for poverty of heart, will see God and obtain the good things Jesus promises. They will enjoy a more abundant life here and an everlasting, perfect life hereafter.

Catechism #2534-2557

A Look into the Heart

1. How have I experienced the challenges of career and family? Do I think that parents should be full-time homemakers, or should they seek to balance their careers and homemaking?
2. Have I connected environmental efforts with Church teachings, joined saving the earth with sanctifying my heart?

Acknowledgements

After publication of an earlier book on the *Catechism*, my editor Anthony Chiffolo suggested another work on modern vices. I am very grateful to him for that original concept and his preliminary efforts to get it off the ground.

Sue Schuster, also an editor at Liguori Publications, then stepped in, advocated quite strongly on behalf of this book, and greatly enhanced it by her editorial corrections and recommendations. I naturally am indebted to Sue for that support and direction, especially in the face of some demanding time pressures.

Redemptorist Father Robert Pagliari, C.SS.R., has, over the past few years, enthusiastically promoted several of my works. I appreciate that encouragement and his most recent decision to move ahead vigorously with this present volume.

Betty and Paul Drotar, several classes at Christian Brothers Academy in Syracuse, and the three persons on the front cover likewise have my special gratitude.

Finally, Patricia Gale has for almost twenty years faithfully transcribed my handwritten copy onto printed pages and now diskettes. I wish to thank her for such long-term cooperative and competent assistance.

May God bestow upon them and all who read these words a fuller life here and the fullness of life hereafter.

Index

abortion xi, **26**
  partial-birth 26
accessibility 55
addiction **29**, 58
adultery 48
animal rights 57
atheism, practical 3
avarice 77

birth control 47

calumny 64, 68
capital punishment 33
career decisions, importance of 75
chastity 44
children, responsibility of 24
civil disobedience 21, 23
civil war 22
cloning 46
confession, seal of 66
confidentiality 69
conscience xi
conscientious objection 38

death 32, 33
  culture of 33
death penalty 33
deterrence 39
detraction 69
disability 55
dishonesty 58, 67, 69
dissent from official teaching xii
divorce 50
drug abuse 31

earth, care of 77
embryo, human 30
engagement 42
envy 77
Eucharist 29
family, sacredness of 24

gambling 57
genetic engineering 31, 46
genocide 39
gospel of life 26
Gospel of Life, The 27
gossip 69
greed 77

homosexuality 45
hostage taking 31

immigration 22

journalists, responsibility of 65
judgment, rash 68

kidnapping 31

labor relations 59
language, foul 8
law 19
legalism 20
lying 67

marketplace practices 58
marriage 42
  same-sex 45

Mass, obligation to attend 12
medical care, ordinary and extraor-
    dinary 32
military service 38
modesty 72
motives, perfect and imperfect ix

names, sacredness of 9

obedience 20
  blind 39
organ donation 31

pacifism 38
parents, responsibility of
    24, 47, 75
pornography 46
poverty 62
privacy 70
property, ownership of 55

revelation 5
  private 6
  public 5

service of others 15
sexual abuse 49
sexuality 45
  debasement of through
  advertising 73
sin x
social justice 60, 61
stealing 58
stewardship 53
suicide, assisted 32, 35
superstition 5, 6

taxes 21
terrorism 23, 31
torture 31

vocation 76
voting 22

war 38
  civil 22
  just 39
welfare, personal 28
work on Sunday 14